Discovering the Person of Holy Spirit

Discovering the Person of Holy Spirit

Volume 1

Alexys V. Wolf

Cover design by Rebeccacovers of FIVERR
Interior design by Aalissha of FIVERR
Editor Pamela Scholtes

The opinions expressed by the author are those of The Fiery Sword Ministries.

Library of Congress Control Number: 2018900949
Published by The Fiery Sword Publications
Lexington, SC

Published in the United States of America

ISBN: 9781976099045

1. Nonfiction > Religion > Christian Life > Inspirational
2. Nonfiction > Religion > Christian Life > Personal Growth

Table of Contents

Table of Contents

Endorsements

The book series *Discovering the Person of Holy Spirit* by Alexys V. Wolf is a spiritual journey to discover who the Holy Spirit is and the role He plays in our lives. Much like the author, I grew up in a mainstream traditional denomination where the Spirit was stifled. We rarely ever discussed the Spirit. I grew up very uncomfortable with such talk. I praise God that it is no longer true. Scripture tells us that Holy Spirit was sent to dwell within us and to be our Comforter. He lives within us. This is where the Trinity comes in: God the Father, God the Son, and God the Holy Spirit. Much of what Mrs. Wolf leads the reader toward is total submission to the will of the Lord. Let's face it: most of us are not sure we want to submit. In fact, we know we don't want to submit; it seems to be against our human nature. We want to be independent and self-sufficient. What we have forgotten is that God created everything and without Him we would not be here. The author defines who the Spirit is and the role He plays in our lives. She writes, "The common Christian has become desensitized about the spirit-realm and its validity in today's society." Wolf points out that Satan has accomplished his task by desensitizing Christians. Mrs. Wolf's book series, *Discovering the Person of Holy Spirit,* is well-organized and well-researched. She uses much Scripture to back her thesis. She ends each chapter with a prayer. This book's format is a reference guide. I can see many uses for this book. First, the average Christian would greatly benefit from the knowledge between the front and back cover. Secondly, pastors and teachers would find this book a great resource for their lessons. Mrs. Wolf obviously spent much time in research and definitely knows her subject. This is one book Christians do not want to miss. ~**Anne B. of Reader's Favorite International Awards Contest**

God brought Alexys into my life only a few years ago, but in those few years I have witnessed what a beautiful work God has done in and through her life. I have had the privilege of observing Him mature her into a vessel through which Holy Spirit can move freely. I have been blessed to be the recipient of hearing the revelations God has shown her. This book series, *Discovering the Person of Holy Spirit*, is a marvelous revelation of those years she spent seeking His heart to me personally. Those truly seeking to know Holy Spirit will find Him as they read this God-inspired book series. May God bless each reader with the supernatural ability to comprehend exactly *who* He is and how Holy Spirit moves in the Earth. ~**Pam Scholtes, Florida**

It is my strong opinion that Alexys' book series, *Discovering the Person of Holy Spirit*, is the best of all her books. I found it not only wonderful but excellent and fantastic. *Discovering the Person of Holy Spirit* has Bible Scriptures as well as names of other author's you might be interested in reading. There are also prayers throughout the chapters that you can say and I said them all. This wonderfully fantastic book series will bring you closer to God. They tell you so many extraordinary things and also not so wonderful things; but the not so wonderful things are a teaching tool. When you reads these books, not only will they help you get closer to God and find out how to get His Spirit, but Alexys also talks openly about some of her personal experiences. After reading those, I loved her all the more. I believe all Christians and non-Christians alike should read this book series. If you are a non-believer, read them and I guarantee you will turn your life over to God and ask Jesus in to your life. I have been a born-again Christian for over 10 years. Although I read my Bible every day, reading these book helps to clarify things from the Bible that I did not understand before. I have learned a lot from Alexys and all of her books but, by far, this one is the best as I find these extremely special. Please, everyone out there be you man or woman, you really have to get this book series. You will be so happy and thrilled that you did. ~ **Cheryl Ann Kelly, Arnprior, Ontario**

Foreword

Alexys is about to take you on a journey. *Discovering the Person of Holy Spirit* book series not like any book I have ever read about Holy Spirit. I am not even sure if I would call them books; they are a reference, a study guide, and a testimony of the very heart and character of God. *Discovering the Person of Holy Spirit* takes you deeper into the word of God than most would endeavor. Alexys has a way of breaking it down and feeding you line upon line, precept upon precept. *Discovering the Person of Holy Spirit* books are foundational, yet a tender haul over the coals for the intellectual who thinks he may have "read it all". Subtly, she will eliminate every excuse you have to not walk fully in His will for your life and eradicate the very justification you thought you had for not knowing and walking in His word. I believe she actually writes, *"Partial surrender is really equal to rebellion"*.

Accepting who we are and then understanding who we are with Holy Spirit is a revelation that can only come from "knowing" His word and Him personally. Alexys ensures that accurate interpretation is expressed and her findings are explored thoroughly. She dissects Scripture within the Word of God, digging deeper into the original intent and language. She leads us with assurance leaving no room for uncertainty.

There comes a point in each of our lives…a *kairos* moment; a point in time that extraordinarily changes you, one that can't be defined by human efforts, and one that couldn't be expected. I believe at one point while reading this expose' on Scripture, you will have your defining moment. You will begin a sentence and by the time you are finished, you will be altered. It's not by anything that Alexys can say but rather how she aims you to His Truth. Like an arrow, you are about to be thrust headfirst into a deeper knowledge of a source so powerful and a supply so sweet that, not only will *you* be changed, but *those around you* will have an encounter because of your experience.

It's not unreasonable to believe we can keep ourselves unstained from the world, that we can walk in love and be a sweet aroma unto the Lord, if we have an understanding of Holy Spirit – if we "know" Him. Let us not be deceived into thinking that He can be separated from Truth, love or God's Word. There is no righteousness apart from Him; *you* cannot tame your tongue without Holy Spirit, and you cannot please God without Him.

Above all else, you cannot decide what parts of Him you want, accept, or believe. You may want to think twice before continuing to read any further. Whether you are ready or not, you are about to be changed. His word is powerful and Alexys has filled these pages with His word, His interpretation and His Truth – Truth convicts and transforms.

There is no need to find a place on your bookshelf for this book series. The moment I finished, I wanted to go back to page one and begin again. If you are like I, you will want to be sure your hi-lighters are full of ink and pen is in hand. Don't get too comfortable. *Discovering the Person of Holy Spirit* will bring you to your knees; it will bring you to a place of repentance, a place of desperation and true freedom. Oh, and I should probably warn you that the passion that Alexys carries is largely contagious.

I pray each person who picks up *Discovering the Person of Holy Spirit*, any volume, will be completely transformed by the renewing of their mind. I pray that each one of us will be open to Your complete Truth, Lord; that not one of us would attempt to be wise in our own eyes. I come against any distractions so that each person may encounter Holy Spirit on a personal level while reading this book. Have Your way, Lord and lead us in paths of righteousness. Teach us Your ways, draw us near to You. I pray that it will be every reader's earnest desire to fall so desperately in love with You that we will draw nearer than ever; so wrapped and coiled that those around us cannot tell where You begin and we end. Change us, God, mold us and transform us. Let our hearts beat as one with Yours.

I thank you, Jesus, for Alexys and her pursuit of You. I thank You for her desire to build Your house *first*. Bless her, Lord, for her desires to see Your people walk in Your Truth and the freedom that accompanies it. Bless her, Father, for her pursuit of righteousness and for her walk of obedience at any cost. I thank You that your will be done and that Your Word will not return void. Thank you for all that You are and for all that You have done for us already. Amen.
~Written by Carrie L. King, Kingston, Ontario

Introduction

"I will lead the blind by a way they do not know, in paths they do not know. I will guide them; I will make darkness into light before them and rugged places into plains. These are the things I will do, and I will not leave them undone (Isaiah 42:16)."

Have you ever wondered the purpose of the Holy Spirit? Growing up in a standard denominational church, I only heard the name "*Holy Spirit*" at water baptism. I rarely heard His name mentioned outside baptism lest they glossed over it while reading the Scriptures. I spent countless years as a born-again believer never knowing how Holy Spirit indwelled believers of Christ.

There is a vast difference between being a born-again believer on the way to heaven and being a born-again believer on the way to heaven with the grand bonus of understanding the fullness of Christ living inside. If you have accepted Christ as Savior, you can learn how to accept Him as Lord by getting to know Holy Spirit allowing Him lordship over your entire being. By granting Holy Spirit full access to your mortal body, there is far greater ease in the "*doing*" of the Word because Holy Spirit is exacting the doing.

Holy Spirit is the deposit or the "*down payment*" of God before He returns for His bride. He is the One in us activating and enabling the power and authority of God to operate in spiritual gifts; to pull down negative thoughts the enemy throws at us; to live a life of love and forgiveness that otherwise is beyond human capability. Holy Spirit is the One within allowing us supernatural ability to discern lies from truth and the wicked from the righteous; to allow us transition from chaos and fear to supernatural peace, faith, and joy.

A vessel is only worth the content it carries.
No matter how beautifully designed or it's outward appearance,
Its value is the matter within.
A thirsty man values a bottle of water.
The bottle itself is useless,
but since it carries that which the man requires,
The water lends value to the bottle.
Yet, if the bottle will not open, both are useless,
no fault of the water.
Likewise, mankind is utterly worthless;
An earthen vessel limited in every way.
When we carry Holy Spirit,
He whom we contain grants mankind all worth.
If, however, we do not allow Him liberty to move through us,
We render both ourselves and Holy Spirit useless —
no fault lies on Holy Spirit.

~Alexys V. Wolf

Chapter 1

A Lie Satan Told Me

Disappointing God:

> "For He was foreknown before the foundation of the world,
> but has appeared in these last times for the sake of you who
> through Him are believers in God, who raised Him from the
> dead and gave Him glory, so that your faith and hope are in
> God (I Peter 1:20-21)."

Some of the most common phrases I hear from people are, *"I just don't want to disappoint God. I don't want to make a mistake. Why would He work through me — I'm so unworthy. I don't know His will, so I'll do nothing."* Not only are these lies we tell ourselves and others, but they are also copouts.

The entire human race already disappointed God before the Earth's foundation to the point He sacrificed the life of His only Son. Now, post-cross, the way we can definitely disappoint God is to never make a concise decision. If we make a wrong decision and it equals sin, be aware the sin debt is already paid. There is no more sacrifice for sin.

Lance Wallnau says that goats always make decisions because they know exactly where they want to go. On the other hand, sheep never decide anything because they don't want to make a mistake. Lack of movement causes stagnation in our spiritual walk and leaves us open prey to the enemy. Stagnation causes atrophy [locked joints], and atrophy causes a slow painful death. We can deduce that not making a decision is a decision to not step out in faith in Christ.

Indeed, I am not talking about flying by the seat of our pants, but walking in the discernment of God's leading. When He opens a door, step through. To say we don't want to make a mistake presses one to make the mistake of missing God's plan. It is actually false humility [pride]. Then, when things go wrong, we blame God. God does not always speak an audible word. Sometimes, He wants us to distinguish between that which is holy and wise or unholy and unwise. This comes from drawing near unto His presence. He expects His bride to seek and function in wisdom.

We Are All Unworthy:

"All of us like sheep have gone astray, each of us has turned to his own way; But the Lord has caused the iniquity of us all to fall on Him (Isaiah 53:6)."

But we have this treasure in Earthen vessels, so that the surpassing greatness of the power will be of God and not from ourselves; we are afflicted in every way, but not crushed; perplexed, but not despairing; persecuted, but not forsaken; struck down, but not destroyed; always carrying about in the body the dying of Jesus, so that the life of Jesus also may be manifested in our body. For we who live are constantly being delivered over to death for Jesus' sake, so that the life of Jesus also may be manifested in our mortal flesh. So death works in us, but life in you (II Corinthians 7:4-12).

All we like sheep have gone astray. The average believer has gone astray because they do not want to sacrifice themselves to God. Most are too afraid He will do something we don't like, take away something we want to keep, send us someplace we don't want to go, or make us do something we don't want to do. I regularly hear these and a litany of other excuses. When people say anything like this, it is merely a lack of submission to God.

Furthermore, to say we are unworthy is correct. Hence it is not allowed as a valid excuse for doing nothing. Not a single person from any generation has ever possessed worth of our own because we are born tainted by Adam's sinful bloodline. It is imperative to recognize that Christ exclusively is our worth and nothing of us. I am just as unworthy as the rest, yet I realize there is a God-plan for His Kingdom. All I need to do is get over myself allowing His will and perfection to pour through me. The same applies to the rest of God's chosen people. If we had even an ounce of self-worth, Jesus could have done something less than give His life's blood.

In recognizing our worthless estate and not internalizing it catapulting us into emotional distress, we can perceive Kingdom facts. In this, we can get over ourselves becoming consumed by God and His righteousness. The entire world telling us to have self-esteem is a lie straight from hell. Self-esteem, self-worth, and things of the like, though they sound great, are nothing short of Satan attempting to distract man from God. Those hidden in Christ should never hone in on *self*, good or bad, barring only self-control and self-discipline. Contrarily, we should set our gaze on the complete worth of God and His life that is alive through our earthen vessel. God-esteem and God-worth should be our only focus.

Desperate for God:

"Come to Me, all who are weary and heavy-laden, and I will give you rest (Matthew 11:28)."

"And we know that God causes all things to work together for good to those who love God, to those who are called according to *His* purpose (Romans 8:28)."

A friend told God she *"wanted to want"* to read the Word, and because of that, He should make it easy for her. What a preposterous notion! To start any statement with, *"He should just…"* is always a bad sign of where we are not with God and our evident self-absorption. God gives instruction to the sheep, not the other way around.

My friend finally admitted that, just maybe, she liked her flesh too much. Keep in mind this is someone who lives a good life in the eyes of the world and church. She doesn't drink, smoke, curse, cheat, etc., the basic church-going Christian. She said, *"Well, I prayed for a while for God to give me a desire to read His Word."* But, after a few days, she gave up. God wants us to see how much we genuinely long for Him.

If a small child says, "*I want a glass of water*," when we are preoccupied flippantly commenting, "*Okay*," with no action, they ask again. We comment again in the same manner. But, when the child begins insisting unrelentingly that they must have a glass of water, only then do we respond. We oblige due to their persistence. They, in a sense, persuaded us to recognize their urgency, and we were moved by their tenacity.

We are the child, and He has the water—*is* the Water. How much do we long for the Water of the Word, to be in an authentic relationship with Him? Do we ask once or twice and then give up? Or are we intensely desperate for God? Do we seek Him to reveal Himself to us letting Him know we will settle for nothing less than knowing His heart? He already knows our hearts. Do we? My friend finally came to the realization she felt she was "*off the hook*" by blaming God for not making her love His Word. Surely it must be His fault. Any time we peg the blame on God for something wrong, a lie is afoot.

There are people throughout the Word absolutely desperate for God. No one had to convince them that God was their only hope. Therefore, in good times and in bad, they lived, "*I am hungry for You, Lord, every hour of every day. I am weary and heavily burdened, yet I can do all things through Christ who gives me strength. Because I find refuge in You, all things will work for my good and the good of Your great Kingdom.*"

Created to Love God:

> "And you shall love the Lord your God with all your heart, and with all your soul, and with all your mind, and with all your strength: this is the first commandment (Mark 12:30, KJV)."

Anyone who thinks their purpose in this life is to get people saved, preach, teach, know and operate in their spiritual gifts or any *"work"* of any kind—not excluding worshiping Him, they are mistaken. This way of thinking is a lie to distract God's people from true intimacy with Him. He is a righteous, holy, majestic, magnificent God. He created everything. He created us, and, in His sovereignty, He created us to love Him, to commune with Him without ceasing.

Once we begin to focus on falling into the heart of God, all the other things will fall into place. Of course, we are to serve and worship Yahweh in many different capacities, but our focus is to love Him and, in our love, obey His commands. A person in love with God can't help but worship Him—it's a supernaturally natural reaction. To worship Him because it's *"the right thing to do"* is virtually worthless.

What more could Yeshua have done besides leaving the written Word, His Holy Spirit, and His peace; giving His Son to brutality and death to pay for our wickedness? He did not say, *"I will love you if you love Me first,"* or *"I will bless you if you do everything perfectly."* He does not ask for our perfection as we have none to offer. He loves us implicitly. Therefore, He asks for our willingness to sacrifice the totality of ourselves so that He may be able to love us and, through that love, move effortlessly through us.

If we grasp the simple fact of having a love-relationship with the Great I AM, we will begin to understand we are not here to work for God. We are here to love and commune with Him and, in turn, rule the Earth on His behalf, just the same as Adam pre-fall. This is why we must allow Him full reign *as* our life—not just *in* your life, so His wisdom and righteousness are permitted to rule. Falling in love with the God [who is love] allows all this to manifest.

By coming to the place of praying, *"Your will be done—no matter what,"* allows Holy Spirit to do the work through our mortal bodies. All God wants us to do is rest in His unfailing love. By resting and allowing Holy Spirit to accomplish His completed work, there is no chance of disappointing Him. It disappoints Him when we run around the local church doing, doing, and doing in His holy name, never stopping to find out who He really is. I hear, *"I know God wants me to do something. I just don't know what it is."*

Most assuredly, God wants us to do something. The *"something"* is to seek His face and fall in love with Him with all our heart, soul, mind, and strength. When we do, if we are a prophet, He will prophesy through us; a healer, He will heal through us; a pastor, He will preach through us, and so on. God has completed His work. There's no more work to be accomplished. We need to get out of His way and allow His completed work to manifest through us.

Notes

Chapter 2

More Lies I Once Believed

I'm Holy Enough:

"For the Scriptures say, 'You must be holy because I am holy (I Peter 1:16, NLT).'"

You were running well; who hindered you from obeying the truth? This persuasion did not come from Him who calls you. A little leaven leavens the whole lump of dough (Galatians 5:7-9).

This thing of "*I'm holy enough. I do a lot of stuff for God. I don't need to spend intimate time with God because of all I accomplish in His name.*" These are lies we have believed far too long. The average believer gets so caught up in their calling they miss the One who called, which brings us back to the sheep always going astray. The individual sheep never learn the voice of the Good Shepherd. Therefore, they never revive clear direction. They don't know the difference between the voice of God, the voice of Satan, and the voice of the flesh.

The goats [those of the world] are trampling over the sheep [the Body of Christ] because the goats have drive and determination. They are led by the evil one who understands determination and drive. It is disgraceful that those led by Satan are more determined to do his will than the Body of Christ is willing to do the will of the Father. Most want to call themselves a good Christian, but they don't want to forsake all to become pure as He is pure. There is no one good except the Father. Jesus said, "*Why do you speak of what is good? Only God is good.*" Focusing on the "*stuff*" of God can become just as sinful as any blatantly sinful conduct we allow in our lives.

The majority do not want to be holy. Instead, they put on a show for the world and the church, yet are not really surrendered. If my friend, referenced earlier, was prostrate before God, she would not cease seeking God until He revealed Himself to her. He is the only pure One. Only His purity functioning through us will make us pure.

God strongly, earnestly desires to reveal Himself to His people. However, He will not waste His precious Word on those who will waste, abandon, or abuse it. If we are too lazy to continually press in to Him, we are likely too lazy to properly apply what He has to offer. Harsh? Yes. True? Yes. The more we seek His face and holiness, the more we will appreciate His Word when we receive all He has for us. If He could make it any easier than He already has, He probably would. But, for me, I'm glad He made me dig in my heels and settle for nothing less than intimate friendship. He wants us to demand nothing less than all of Him. We will be the ones who benefit.

What if I Can't Do It?

"Not that we are adequate in ourselves to consider anything as coming from ourselves, but our adequacy is from God (II Corinthians 3:5)."

Abide in Me, and I in you. As the branch cannot bear fruit of itself unless it abides in the vine, so neither can you unless you abide in Me. I am the vine, you are the branches; he who abides in Me and I in him, he bears much fruit, for apart from Me you can do nothing (John 15:3-5).

Let's face it. We are going to make mistakes from time to time. No one is exempt. Don't we realize the Lord knows this and will work all things together for good when we love Him? It is a promise on which He cannot go back. He did it for all those who went before you; the disciples, David, Moses, Abraham, Isaac, Jacob, Elijah, and countless others. They were not without flaws. In fact, they were fully flawed. That's how He was able to prove Himself and, in turn, able to glorify Himself instead of the person.

David was called a *"man after God's own heart,"* yet he was a terrible disciplinarian when it came to his children. He became an adulterer, liar, manipulator, and murderer with a horrific temper. God sent Nathan to bring a verdict of death to David. In so doing, he recognized his heart's poor condition and repented. God never called David for his perfection as he made mistakes—big ones. What if David, as a boy, had been indecisive about slaying the giant? By human standards, there was no way David could accomplish the task. What if he had said, *"Well, I don't want to disappoint God. What if I fail?"* History would be different.

It was counted unto Abraham as righteousness for his faith yet, when he did not initially get a son in the timing he deemed appropriate, he agreed to sleep with another woman. That doesn't sound like much faith in God to me. In time, however, he did what was right in the sight of God through faith, and God gave him Isaac by his wife, Sarah. God did not call him to perfection, just a willing, humble heart to obey. What if Abraham said at 100 that he refused to have relations with Sarah because they were too tired and there was no way she would get pregnant? Most people at 100 have no desire for sex—that is, if they are still living. Nevertheless, in faith that God would fulfill His word, he did, she did, and God did. He made a decision. God fulfilled His promise through their faithfulness.

The widow woman and her son were almost out of flour. The prophet came and said, *"Bake for me first and then for you and your son."* What if she said something like, *"Well, I know there won't be enough, and I don't want to disappoint God by baking bad bread. His servant won't like it."* She would have died along with her son, and God would not have been able to reveal His wondrous miracle, power, and grace through the situation.

I Was Born This Way:

"Therefore if anyone is in Christ, he is a new creature; the old things passed away; behold, new things have come. (II Corinthians 5:17)."

But I say, walk by the Spirit, and you will not carry out the desire of the flesh. For the flesh sets its desire against the Spirit, and the Spirit against the flesh; for these are in opposition to one another, so that you may not do the things that you please (Galatians 5:16-17)."

"I was born this way" is a topic common to everyone at some juncture. The thought process of *"I was born this way, so I'll always be this way"* or *"I was born this way, God must want me this way"* is most definitely a lie breathed from Satan's lips. It can reference a bad attitude, anger, sloth, lying, cheating, fearfulness, bullying, and even homosexuality. I have heard, *"God don't make no junk,"* which, in my estimation, people of this mindset think we're all born into perfection and, inevitably, muddy ourselves along the way. Contrary to this belief, we are all born as *"junk"* [a worthless earthen vessel] in so much as we are all born naturally into the old Adamic nature [Adam's tainted bloodline].

I know children who tend to be pathological liars right out of the womb. I know people who are angry from birth, depressed from birth, and, yes, have a predisposition to homosexuality from birth. I don't understand why we act so surprised and attempt to deny how we are naturally born. The natural man never accomplished or produced anything good dating back to The Fall of man. Since we come from Adam and Adam was declared dead while he remained physically alive, all he could bear is death. Hence, we are all dead at conception.

This being so, we should expect our natural man to be tainted, impure, and unholy. Our thoughts, words, and deeds are corrupt from conception. Accepting this simple truth is what will drive us to the very place of being desperate for God, desperate for His re-demptive blood leading us to utterly consign the old nature to God desiring to be positioned to receive regeneration from God through Jesus. In Christ, we now have a brand new bloodline enabling us to stop being how we were born from our natural parents. With the newness [regeneration], we can be everything God called and created us to be—no excuses no matter how we came into existence.

If you or I, for instance, were born naturally with homosexual tendencies, but are now reborn in the perfection of God, that does not mean we will suddenly be attracted to the opposite sex. Alter-nately, it means that we choose a holy path regardless of what the dead fleshly man may desire. This is the war between the flesh and the Spirit. This is counting all as loss and living a life of *"losing all things."* To truly consign ourselves spirit, soul, and body to the majes-ty of God, we will see the *"loss of a homosexual relationship"* as nothing compared to all God gave to rescue us from eternal hell.

Furthermore, the new life God gave to ensure us a place in the Kingdom of heaven, even while on Earth, far outweighs anything we must submit. The price we pay pales in comparison to the ultimate sacrifice He extended. Stop believing the lie. Unless it is about how and in whom we have been spiritually born, we must pull this think-ing away from our minds and hearts.

> For those who are according to the flesh set their minds on the things of the flesh, but those who are according to the Spirit, the things of the Spirit (Romans 8:5)."

But whatever things were gain to me, those things I have counted as loss for the sake of Christ. More than that, I count all things to be loss in view of the surpassing value of knowing Christ Jesus my Lord, for whom I have suffered the loss of all things, and count them but rubbish so that I may gain Christ, and may be found in Him, not having a righteousness of my own derived from *the* Law, but that which is through faith in Christ, the righteousness which *comes* from God on the basis of faith, that I may know Him and the power of His resurrection and the fellowship of His sufferings, being conformed to His death; in order that I may attain to the resurrection from the dead (Philippians 3:7-11).

Prayer:

Our most gracious Savior, hallowed be Thy name in all the Earth. Continually show me Your will that I may step in faith when You open the doorway. Open every door that no man can close, and close every door that no man can open. Teach me Your ways, O God, that I become so merged with You that I won't flinch in the face of the enemy. I will no longer be led by fear of failure. I thank You, Christ my Sovereign, that as my heart is set on You, You will lead, guide, direct, and orchestrate my path every step of the way through Holy Spirit. I surrender spirit, soul and body to Your Spirit. I freely give myself to you. May nothing and no one hinder Your sovereignty. Selah

Notes

Chapter 3

The Young Prophet

Intimidation:

Be [a command, an action word] strong and very courageous…do [action word] not let this Book of the Law depart
from your mouth [know the Word]; meditate on it day and
night, so that you may be careful to do everything written in
it. Then you will be prosperous and successful. Have I not
commanded you? Be strong and courageous. Do not be ter-
rified; do not be discouraged, for the Lord your God will be
with you wherever you go [this is a promise] (Joshua 1:7-9).

Definition of Intimidation:
1. to make timid; fill with fear
2. to overawe or cow, as through the force of personality or by
   superior display of wealth, talent, etc.
3. to force into or deter from some action by inducing fear

*I*ntimidation is a tool of the devil to stop God's work through mankind. *"For God did not give us a spirit of timidity, but a spirit of power, of love and self-discipline,"* reads II Timothy 1:7. I John 4:18 states, *"There is no fear in love. But perfect love casts out fear because fear has to do with punishment. The one who fears is not made perfect in love."*

If there is any area of life causing us to fear or be discouraged, our flesh is still active, and it needs to be submitted or resubmitted to Holy Spirit. A dead man knows no offense, no fear, no discouragement, and no intimidation. We are commanded to take up our cross daily remembering we entered into co-death with Jesus when He crucified the fleshly nature of all mankind. Intimidation comes from viewing ourselves from the natural perspective instead of God's supernatural perspective.

The cross represents both death and life. We cannot serve two masters. God, through Holy Spirit, communes with our spirit, but Satan works through the flesh and soul since he cannot touch our spirit. We either serve the flesh [Satan] or the Spirit [God]. Colossians 3:3 reads, *"For you died, and your life is now hidden with Christ in God."*

The blood of Jesus washes over the flesh, soul, and Holy Spirit within. This way, He is *in* us, *on* us, and *through* us. Holy Spirit [our new life] cannot be intimidated, so what right do we have to give life back to the flesh, allowing it to fall prey to intimidation? A few symptoms of intimidation and fear are:

1. self-pity
2. depression
3. confusion
4. loss of spiritual vision

5. discouragement
6. timidity
7. distraction
8. inability to pray
9. thinking more highly of ourselves than we ought
10. double-mindedness

We need to always remember that these are only physical manifestations, not the root cause. The root of the symptoms is the nature of the flesh stemming from cursed Adam. If the natural man has not been consigned to Holy Spirit, though saved from hell, we have not been set free from the lures of the flesh.

This is why people go through years of counseling spending thousands of dollars on medication for problems, yet never get set free. The root of all issues is *spiritual*, not *physical*, yet, with futility, we attempt to deal with topical issues as though they are merely physical. The root cannot be pulled up and plucked out because the natural cannot correctly assess or address the spiritual. Many of God's strongest confronted with intimidation were Moses, David, Elijah, Elisha, Mary, Joseph, and others with whom we are familiar. I would like, however, to draw attention to a less known young man named Elihu found in the book of Job.

We must be exceedingly careful to recognize intimidation when the devil throws it our way, and he will. The entire book of Job is about being led by Holy Spirit. In everything we do, Holy Spirit is the only road to a successful, powerful, and courageous life in Christ. Although Job was a righteous man [perfect, as God himself refers to Job], he was not sinless. In other words, *"perfect"* means his bloodline was not tainted by the sins of the wicked around him. He was pure before God as was Noah. Because of Job's hidden sin, Elihu, a young prophet, was sent to call him to accountability. Although I spoke extensively about this in *Looking for God, volume II*, I'll recap briefly.

Job's Hidden Fear:

> "For what I fear comes upon me, and what I dread befalls me (Job 3:25)."

There's that dreaded word—*fear*. It is a pitfall for every Christ-follower who gives in to it. Fear indicates Job's faith was not entirely in the Lord. Fear was hidden, even from Job.

Now his so-called friends come along accusing him of having secret sin, which Job vehemently denied. He stood firmly that he had nothing hidden. Denial is a common manifestation stemming from deep-seated pride. As they accuse Job, he turns and accuses them.

> "For the despairing man there should be kindness from his friend; so that he does not forsake the fear of the Almighty. My brothers have acted deceitfully like a wadi, like the torrents of wadis which vanish (Job 6:14-15)."

> "What you know I also know; I am not inferior to you. But I would speak to the Almighty, and I desire to argue with God (Job 13:2-3)."

"The fear of the Lord—that is wisdom, and to shun evil is understanding (Job 28:28)."

Notice Job sought flattery, kind words to stroke his ego making him feel better. We should never be dependent on the flattering words of others to make us feel good. If we are confident in ourselves instead of who we are in Christ, we will surely crumble and perish. This banter goes back and forth for many chapters. Job goes on endlessly defending himself. They eluded there was a possibility Job was harboring something sinful deeply within.

Job and his three friends each knew the principles of God, but their knowledge was strictly intellectual. By chapter 29, Job begins to speak of all the wonderful things he had done. He begins to absolutely exude pride. Here is a snippet:

> For when the ear heard, it called me blessed, and when the eye saw, it gave witness of me, because I delivered the poor who cried for help, and the orphan who had no helper. The blessing of the one ready to perish came upon me, and I made the widow's heart sing for joy. I put on righteousness, and it clothed me; my justice was like a robe and a turban (Job 29:11-14, 23-24).

Notes

Chapter 4

A Man without Fear

So these three men stopped answering Job, because he was righteous in his own eyes. But Elihu became very angry with Job for justifying himself rather than God. He was also angry with the three friends, because they had found no way to refute Job, and yet had condemned him (Job 32:1-3).

*E*nter Elihu. He was obviously present during the debate between Job and his friends, yet he sat ever so quietly. He had a word from God to speak to all four men, but he waited until the proper time. Elihu was much younger than they. He could have been easily intimidated to the point of silence, yet God clearly sent him to speak as an ambassador from the Kingdom of Heaven. Elihu was filled with and led by Holy Spirit, not his flesh. If he'd been fleshly, it would have caused him to cower in fear in the presence of his elders. He was not intimidated, nor did he shrink in fear. He knew all too well the One from whom he was sent.

Why was Elihu mad with Job's three friends? Was it because they were wrong in their accusations? No, it was because they were right,

The good people. thing? [handwritten annotation in top margin]

but they were too spiritually ignorant to know why they were right or how to reveal Job's sin in the spirit of love. They were utterly self-righteous, as was Job. They passed judgment and condemnation instead of being driven by Holy Spirit to help instruct Job into purity. This is the current state of affairs among the brethren. They point out people's flaws to condemn. It should be that, if we are called to address someone's flaws, do so with a heart of love to bring them out of their sin.

Job and his three friends' thoughts, ideas, and actions were instructed by their intellect and head-knowledge. They had no connection with Holy Spirit. How many people run around aimlessly trying to *"get people saved,"* telling people everything wrong with them, and then how great they are themselves? Intellectual knowledge of God is not the wisdom of God, nor is its intimacy with Him. Anyone can study and memorize the Word, never allowing it to penetrate the very core of their being. Chapter after chapter, we witness Job and his friends speaking truthful factoids *about* God, yet they did not express a deep, intimate relationship with Him.

Remember Job 28:28? Job spoke of true wisdom he did not possess. Only those led by the Spirit of God can walk in truth allowing God to work through them. Job's friends were unrelenting for a time, then they grew weary and gave up because their words were of the mind and not of the heart of the Spirit of God. Elihu was mad with Job because he was so caught in his own greatness that he became bloated with pride smothering all humility. Because of Job's pride, he became rebellious against God—pride always ushers rebellion. Rebellion always acts out through the person like, *"You can't tell me I'm wrong. I am as good as you. Who do you think you are?"*

God gives grace to the humble. No humility, no grace. David suffered greatly in the wilderness when he fled from Saul and Absalom. Notwithstanding, he remained humble receiving great grace. Job had sins [pride, fear, and rebellion] that weren't brought to light until devastation hit. Job 1:5 states, "*And it came about, when the days of feasting had completed their cycle, that Job would send and consecrate them, rising up early in the morning and offering burnt offerings according to the number of them all; for Job said, 'Perhaps my sons have sinned and cursed God in their hearts.' Thus Job did continually.*" Job was perpetually afraid for his children, so much that he sacrificed on their behalf and he didn't have the power to do that. He could not atone for someone else's sin. This was blatant fear and idolatry on Job's part.

Elihu Speaks:

...I am young in years, and you are old...I must open my lips and reply. I will show partiality to no one, nor will I flatter any man; for if I were skilled in flattery, my Maker would soon take me away (Job 32:6, 21-22).

"For he adds rebellion to his sin; he claps his hands among us, and multiplies his words against God (Job 34:37)."

When we genuinely love someone in crisis, we would not spend time flattering them trying to make them feel better about themselves. Instead, we tell our loved one the truth so they will be adequately instructed on how to end the crisis and grow from it. Frequently, though the truth is spoken in love, it is uncomfortable. Consigning dead flesh over to God is never comfortable. Death hurts. The Truth reveals the flesh and all its cancerous growths to be adequately equipped to separate flesh and soul [mind, will, emotions] from the spirit [our true self].

Elihu, although a young man and seemingly inexperienced, refused to give way to intimidation. He spoke with the power and authority of the Almighty. He expressed the wisdom of God through Holy Spirit for six chapters, and then God spoke. It was painful for Job to hear what Elihu had to say and even more painful to hear what God had to say. Job was incredibly humbled and finally recognized his sins of pride, fear, and rebellion. In his condition of humility, he repented as dust and ashes.

I heard it said that God deals with people better in judgment than in blessings because that is when we best respond. Too often, when blessed abundantly as was Job, we do not hear Him. In trouble, however, we will surely take stock to see how to get out of distress.

Intimidation Quenches Holy Spirit:

Notice the similarity between what God says of Satan and what God says of Job: "*You* [Lucifer] *had the seal of perfection. Full of wisdom and perfect in beauty…you were blameless in your ways from the day you were created until unrighteousness was found in you…*(Ezekiel 28:12, 15)." Job 1:1 (KJV) reads, "*There was a man…Job; and that man was perfect and upright…*"

Unfortunately, both Job and Lucifer were described very similarly by God. The only difference between the two is that Satan did not relent in his wickedness but, once Elihu and God spoke truth to Job,

Job did relent, humbled himself, and repented. Only then was he doubly blessed.

This life-change in Job would not have occurred had Elihu given in to intimidation and fear of speaking with authoritative Holy Spirit power. If Elihu had caved in the face of intimidation coming from those older than him and had not spoken, God would not have spoken. If God had not spoken, Job would not have seen his own sin and, therefore, would not have known of what to repent. Elihu knew he had the gift of wisdom and insight allowing Holy Spirit to work and speak through him. History would be vastly different had Elihu cowered in fear of what the men would think of him.

"My ears had heard of You but now my eyes have seen You. Therefore I despise myself and repent in dust and ashes," declares Job in chapter 42, verses 5-6. When we really experience God, we will be completely broken and humbled. There will be nothing left of us to boast. *"Dust and ashes"* refers to death to himself [his fleshly nature] that drove him to demand God explain Himself. Now Job was able to live a poured-out life for Yeshua.

There is so much more in this lesson far exceeding spiritual intimidation. We need to understand that spiritual intimidation and fear hinder the work of the Lord through us. Elihu could have been intimidated by age, lavish words, long speeches, experiencing rejection, or the experience and head-knowledge of others. Neither Job nor his three friends were led by Holy Spirit. They were all arrogant and foolish in their words, defenses, and accusations. Whatever mission on which we embark, make sure God is doing the sending, not emotions or intellect. God wants us to see in ourselves what He sees to rid ourselves of anything hindering our relationship with Christ.

Desert places are not supposed to be permanent. They are set in place to learn to trust the Lord developing a close, intimate relationship with Father. Remember, nothing comes to our door lest it first pass through the hand and approval of God. Don't look at what Satan is doing. Look at what God is doing.

If we are one, Yeshua has positioned us to speak the truth as He did Elihu, command that spirits of fear and intimidation to leave, replacing them with the boldness, courage, and humility of Jesus. The lives of those around us depend upon our obedience.

Prayer:

Father, I come before You contrite and lowly. I ask that You reveal to me every wicked way and every fruitless deed of darkness that I myself have not seen. May I walk in courage, faith, love, and the strength that stems only from You. Amen.

Notes

Chapter 5

Christ the Lowly

"…thus says the Lord God, 'Remove the turban and take off the crown; this will no longer be the same. Exalt that which is low and abase that which is high (Ezekiel 21:26)."

"Take My yoke upon you, and learn of me; for I am meek and lowly in heart; and ye shall find rest unto your souls (Matthew 11:29, KJV)."

"I dwell on a high and holy place, and also with the contrite and lowly of spirit… (Isaiah 57:15)."

"For though the Lord is exalted, yet He regards the lowly, but the haughty He knows from afar (Psalm 138:6)."

Definition of Lowly:
1. humble in feeling, behavior or status
2. modest; unpretentious
3. evolved to only a slight degree

There was a point where the Lord spoke to me, "*Associate with the lowly.*" I pondered if He was referring to inmates through my prison ministry or people in general. Suddenly, I realized it was a word letting me know that *I* am the lowly. As He is the high and lifted One, He lowered Himself to be as lowliness *like* mankind, *with* mankind, to *reveal* to mankind how to humble ourselves one to another. Basically, He became like you and me, the lowly, so we can become like Him, highly exalted and favored by God.

Since I am the lowly, I keep that image in the forefront of my mind when the flesh in which I dwell wants to arise and lie deceiving me into thinking I am even one ounce better than someone else. Knowing and understanding this concept makes it all the easier to forgive someone before they form an offense against me. I can reach out to people in any walk of life, no matter how much it may not appeal to my flesh.

For instance, I hear all too regularly how people are having a hard time forgiving a parent, child, boss, friend, neighbor, etc., for abusing, neglecting, rejecting, or harming them in some way. They cite they would not be in such a horrible place had that person done better by them. Since their unforgiveness results from judgment, they are having a hard time repenting of both the judgment and unforgiveness, leaving them in an even deeper mess than what the offender did. I am referring to people claiming to walk with God *in* the world, not the ones *of* the world.

There can be no walk with God without forgiveness, repentance, and removal of judgment. By "*judgment,*" I refer to a judgmental spirit, not righteous judgment. I have taught repeatedly on this matter. It is vital to understand and practice forgiveness daily. When we [followers of Christ] can truly begin to see ourselves through the eye [single vision] of God, we will realize we are no better than the one who hurt us. We are also no better than anyone who doesn't walk closely with God. It is a complicated concept to accept, yet it is, without a doubt, a key element in a successful *"Christ living through me"* life. Instead of saying ad nauseam how a person wronged us or how they are simply wrong in their overall life, start saying how gracious Yeshua has been to spare our life when we were not walking correctly. This requires a Kingdom-of-God mindset 24/7/365.

We must look at ourselves with a new Kingdom vision. We must realize how filthy our sins were before God cleansed us. You personally, just as did I, offended Almighty God before we humbled ourselves to receive His gift of salvation. He says that each of us was His enemy when He died and rose again. Jesus allowed pain, sorrow, and death to come upon Himself. He had to face being forsaken by His Father, and He did all this for you and me *before* we were thought of or had ever exerted our first sin. He died for us, knowing we would rebel against Him, and He did it anyway because of His unfailing, unwavering love.

The entire world for every generation is wholly forgiven. In fact, if we are going to be sticklers about it, one should never pray, *"O God, forgive me of this or that."* We are already fully forgiven. What we should pray is something like, *"O gracious God, I repent of* _____, *and I fully receive and apply to my life the forgiveness given to me at the cross of Calvary."*

Forgiveness is not given at your confession. It was given a long time ago. The repentance of sin for a believer is simply an act of humility [lowliness] on our part, which ushers back into our lives the open door to God and His holy Kingdom. In this, we will realize it is actually blasphemy against His death, burial, and resurrection to beat ourselves for our past as though our sins are too terrible for His forgiveness to be sufficient.

Humility of Forgiveness:

Now we come to forgiving others of heinous crimes committed against loved ones or us. It is astonishing how people can walk for many years claiming the grace of God, but they never forgive that one person in their life they deem *"unworthy."* When we begin to see through new spiritual spectacles, our hearts will melt for the offender as God's heart melted for His offender—you and me. It does not mean the offenders were justified in their actions, only that we can now extend mercy and grace as was extended to us.

Mercy is *not* being given something we *do* deserve [punishment]. Grace, on the other hand, is receiving something we *don't* deserve [pardon]. Like the woman in Matthew, the more love we realize we have been given what we do not deserve, the more love we will pour onto those who equally do not deserve it.

Isaiah 57:15, listed at the opening of this chapter, is clear. God abides in two places: *I dwell on a high and holy place* [heaven], *and also with the contrite and lowly of spirit* [the one humbled before God]. When we lower ourselves, we will be lifted up where He resides in the heavenly realm. One cannot be lifted by God lest they first lower themselves. We must see ourselves from God's perspective. When we see ourselves as better than anyone, we have raised ourselves, and we will have to be lowered, either by our own hand or the hand of the

Almighty. The choice is ours as it is for every individual. It's simple mathematics.

Let's say, though, that no one offended or harmed you personally. Maybe they simply have a different skin color, nationality, speech, style, amount of money [less or more], etc. All over the world, there are nations against nations because they don't believe the same way. Do you think yourself better than a Muslim, Buddhist, atheist, Indian, Catholic, Baptist, etc.? My Hispanic friends tell me there is a rivalry between Latinos: Spaniards, Mexicans, Puerto Ricans, etc. What about African Americans where the lighter-skinned people think themselves better than darker-skinned or vice versa? I believe it is called "*colorism.*" Of course, there is the ever-typical white against black. The list of prejudices is a bottomless pit. If you think of yourself better than anyone, it is pride, and God cannot grant you grace.

Notes

Chapter 6

~Brokenness

The First Sin:

"The fear of the Lord is to hate evil: I hate pride and arrogance, evil behavior and perverse speech (Proverbs 8:13)."

"Pride goes before destruction, a haughty spirit before a fall…(Proverbs 16:18)."

"Do you think the Scripture says without reason that the Spirit He caused to live in us envies intensely? But He gives more grace. That is why the Scripture says: 'God opposes the proud, but gives grace to the humble (James 4:5-6).'"

"All of you, clothe yourselves with humility toward one another (I Peter 5:5)."

ride was the first sin. As David E. Taylor points out in His book *Victory Over Pride*, Lucifer manifested the only sin that can enter when everything else is set in order. Pride is the only sin that can attack while in the presence of perfection. Pride is one of the most challenging enemies to see or detect. Scriptures say that pride goes before destruction. That means that pride is not destruction, but is sent as an ambassador before the destruction comes. Pride destroys God's people daily. Things such as rebellion, unforgiveness, rage, malice, slander, boasting, self-abasement, and coveting are a few manifestations of pride. To be frank, anything in the form of rebellion against God's Word all stems from P.R.I. D.E, bar none. All expressions of sin arise from it.

We must allow God to reveal the hidden fruitless deeds of darkness buried deep within us. Pride causes God's grace to be rejected in our lives even though it has been activated in other areas. Grace comes only in the presence of humility. Look at the subsequent passages. Holy Spirit cannot rule when pride rules. It's one or the other.

"I, Nebuchadnezzar, was at home in my palace, contented, and prosperous (Daniel 4:4)."

"While people are saying, 'Peace and safety,' destruction will come on them suddenly, as labor pains on a pregnant woman, and they will not escape (I Thessalonians 5:3)."

Daniel 4 reads that the king, just before the wrath of God came against him, was content in his home. He had no consciousness of God whatsoever, though he had been warned by Daniel. He thought himself superior, self-sufficient, self-sustaining, self-made. He commended his own hand for having brought himself such superiority among the nations. Pride only seems to be suitable for a season, but that season will end abruptly. Destruction came in an instant though it took twelve months to manifest from the time Daniel spoke the prophecy of destruction. Just when Nebuchadnezzar became comfortable in the luxury of his home, the penance of pride arrived. Prideful people rest in their wickedness when they need to be warring against the evil in their midst. Pride would not allow the king to humble himself to repent before God, a decision for which he paid dearly.

It's time for God's royal priesthood to take this application and put it to use in our individual lives. Have *you* allowed pride in your heart? Are *you* allowing pride to destroy your family, job, health, finances, or, more importantly, your relationship with God? If so, begin seeking inwardly allowing God to reveal all pride within. Then expunge it from your person.

Pride is very tricky and manifests differently from person to person. Since it was the first accounted sin, don't think for one moment anyone is exempt. For the one who shows it outwardly, once they become aware of it, it is relatively simple to remove. Contrarily, it is not so easily detected for the rest of the Body of Christ; those doing good deeds, going to church regularly, dressing modestly, not stealing, lying, cursing, drinking, smoking, doing drugs, etc. These are the people most susceptible to the lures of pride. Because Satan is deceptive, he slinks into God's people unawares. He does not come with a forked tail and pitchfork or some ornate Halloween costume—he is beautiful and intensely alluring. II Corinthians 11:14 makes it evident that he masquerades as a beacon of light, as an angel.

Again, to quote David E. Taylor in *Victory Over Pride*, "*Pride always leads you to the high place. Humility leads you to the low place. Pride is whatever makes your head too big for a room...in the world, the leader in a chain of authority is positioned at the top. The pyramid is right side up. Everyone at the bottom serves the one at the top. However, in the Kingdom of God, the pyramid is upside down. The person who is the greatest is servant to all. The pinnacle is still pointing toward the leader, but the leader is at the bottom serving all. Jesus lowered Himself and served others and exalted all others above Himself, including His enemies. Even on the cross, He prayed for those who hung Him."*

World's Authority
Prideful purposing to rise to
glory having others serve them

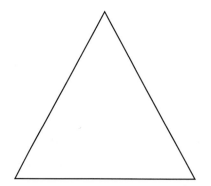
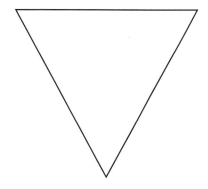

Jesus' Authority
Humbled Himself to serve
others and to love His
neighbor as Himself

Remain Broken:

> But Jesus called them to Himself and said, "You know that the rulers of the Gentiles lord it over them, and their great men exercise authority over them. It is not this way among you, but whoever wishes to become great among you shall be your servant, and whoever wishes to be first among you shall be your slave; just as the Son of Man did not come to be served, but to serve, and to give His life a ransom for many (Matthew 20:26-28).

> "But the greatest among you shall be your servant. Whoever exalts himself shall be humbled; and whoever humbles himself shall be exalted (Matthew 23:11)."

We are not here to be served, but to serve, the same as Jesus since it is Jesus living through us. Those who desire to be great will be brought down. Christ states that those who serve are the greatest among His people, but those who purpose in the name of Christ Jesus to serve the body will be highly exalted in due season. There is a massive difference between a slave and a servant. A *slave* is in bondage to his master with no choice. Therefore, he becomes easily embittered. A *servant,* on the other hand, is employed by choice by his superior. He serves with diligence because his payment is imminent.

A *bondservant* is a person who is released from slavery, yet chooses to remain out of dedication and love. This person is willing to do anything they are asked without hesitation or grudge. God's bond-servants who serve with a grateful heart will be rewarded in the

Kingdom of heaven. The lower we humble ourselves before Christ and mankind, the higher we are moved toward Christ. We become more of a servant as time goes by, not less. This is the way the King and the Father are honored.

Our most significant purpose in this life is to love and glorify the Father. When we are focused on ourselves, we shift the focus from Him. Pride can be very subtle. Remember what I said about those most at risk? It is effortless to find ourselves out of spiritual sync with God because we forget whom we serve and the One who gives us all ability to do what we do. We can easily allow the praises we receive from those around us to puff us internally. Miss Barder, the mentor of the most humble, Watchman Nee, a man of God who suffered intensely for China, spoke this of humility in the book, *Watchman Nee: Sufferer of China*, page 30:

> "Stay broken. Don't believe all the good things people say about you. You must stay broken. His Word says that if your ways are pleasing to the Lord, He will make your enemies to be at peace with you. He is most pleased with your brokenness. Remember the cross, To-sheng (Watchman Nee). You must stay broken."

When we are in a place of servitude, we must remember there is no good but God. Therefore, if there is good coming from us, it is not us, but Christ through our mortal bodies. Human nature tends to look judgmentally on those not doing what we are or conducting themselves and us. To be judgmental comes from a spirit of pride, and no one is exempt; we've all done it at some point. The key is to be so aware that we don't allow it to remain and take root.

We must be quick to repent of a judgmental spirit and remove the foothold of the enemy. Keep in mind that the Body of Christ is to judge things according to the Spirit of God—this is righteous judgment. That differs significantly from being judgmental [viewing ourselves better than another]. God's holy people also need to be careful about starting a "*life story*" wanting to exalt God, yet talk endlessly about ourselves and what *we* did or said in a specific situation. Human nature, once again, is to glorify self getting people to be in awe of how humble and selfless we seem. This is not behavior indicative of Christ revealing that Holy Spirit is not leading.

Notes

Chapter 7

Everyone's Issue

My Definition of Pride:

Pushing
Righteousness
Into
Dire
Elimination

"Take My yoke upon you and learn from me, for I am gentle and humble in heart, and you will find rest for your souls (Matthew 11:29)."

"For if you forgive men when they sin against you, your heavenly Father will also forgive you. But if you do not forgive men their sins, your Father will not forgive your sins (Matthew 6:14-15)."

The Chair:

> "My heavenly Father will also do the same to you, if each of you does not forgive his brother from your heart (Matthew 18:35)."

Obviously, according to the Bible, pride is an issue with which everyone somehow, somewhere needs to confront. Pride requires constant pruning because it grows like weeds and spreads itself as fast and as far as it can. It is unrelenting. Once we deal with pride, we cannot assume it is never to be faced again. Our hearts require constant supervision. The fleshly nature is driven by pride. We all need to be alert to it regularly. We all need to be so heavily clothed in the spirit of humility [Holy Spirit] that we walk in a perpetual internal condition of forgiveness. This translates we are to have forgiveness readily available for those who have not yet offended us.

Many years ago, I was taught how to alleviate unforgiveness and judgment formed against others. The technique is to put people in *"the chair."* The process is to pull up an empty chair imagining the offender is sitting there. Tell them what they have done to hurt, offend, or anger you. Once you have released your irritations, frustrations, and heartache, forgive them from the heart. The next step is to confess to God and repent of all judgment forged against them. Pray and ask God to apply His forgiveness to you for the judgment you've held in your heart against them.

This is an excellent technique for purging oneself of hidden unforgiveness and judgment. Pride is the only thing standing in the way of forgiveness. Getting our own hearts clean is our issue, not whether they hear our plea, receive forgiveness, or apologize for what they did wrong. It really has nothing to do with the other person at all.

People rebut with, *"Well, I think putting people in the chair is a cop-out. I should go to those people every time to repent of my unforgiveness. How they react does not matter, only that I tell them what they did wrong, how it affected me, what is going on with me, and that I forgive them anyway."* Clearly, there are times we should go to an actual person. If the one who hurt or offended us is a friend, they should be able to listen, apologize for their action, and forgive us for whatever we've held in our hearts against them.

That being said, if they are really a friend, the question we should ask ourselves is *"Why am I offended?"* Then we should ask, *"Are they someone that would purposely hurt me?"* If not, consider they did not mean to hurt us and don't let their misstep offend any longer. Otherwise, maybe they aren't someone with whom we need to remain in relationship. We should control our emotions and be slow to anger and offense (Psalm 119:165).

Please understand that putting people in the empty chair strictly keeps our hearts clean before God. The attitude of *"I have to confront the offender"* is erroneous because what may seem humble on our part by confessing to the offender is, in reality, an act of revenge. It is having the perspective of, *"I'm going to tell them what they did to me because they need to know."* However, in actuality, people with this attitude just want to tell the offender what they did wrong so that they will hurt like the offended and recognize how "big" the forgiver is. It's all quite selfish and prideful at heart.

This person's so-called *"confession"* of unforgiveness and judgment to the offender is not an act of humility. In response to such a confession, more anger and judgment are going round and round, now in both people. If the offender did not accept the so-called apology and become angry at the offended, both the offended and the offender grow more furious. By going to the actual person, fire is being fueled when it all could have been avoided simply by keeping mouths closed and dealing with personal issues in our quiet time with Yahweh. This requires genuine humility.

There may be someone attempting to regularly annoy or upset us. In this instance, it is not necessary to go to them every time. If we did, we would irritate the situation by making them irritated. We, then, are the ones making our brother or sister fall, and the guilt lies on us. Be very mindful and discerning about whom to apologize in person or privately to an empty chair. Nine times out of ten, privately is the best resolution.

Remember, the person who has offended may be very fragile in their heart. If we, thinking only of ourselves, go to them when they upset us, we may make them feel worse about themselves because they did not know what they did. Another scenario could be that the offender has confirmation they accomplished their task of annoying us, and they will continue all the more. Some people are full of evil spirits, and it is their mission to wreak as much havoc on others as possible. Be careful with people. We are a fragile creation, and we need tender, loving care that can only be given through obedience to Holy Spirit within.

The Attack of Pride:

You [Lucifer] had the seal of perfection, full of wisdom and perfect in beauty. You were in Eden, the garden of God;

every precious stone was your covering; the ruby, the topaz, and the diamond; the beryl, the onyx, and the jasper; the lapis lazuli, the turquoise and the emerald; and the gold, the workmanship of your settings and sockets, was in you. On the day that you were created they were prepared…your heart became proud on account of your beauty, and you corrupted your wisdom because of your splendor. So I threw you to the Earth; I made a spectacle of you before kings (Ezekiel 28:12-17).

"But when his [King Belshazzar] heart became arrogant and hardened with pride, he was deposed from his royal throne and stripped of his glory (Daniel 5:20)."

See, I will make you small among the nations; you will be utterly despised. The pride of your heart has deceived you, you who live in the clefts of the rocks and make your home on the heights, you who say to yourself, 'Who can bring me down to the ground?' Though you soar like the eagle and make your nest among the stars, from there I will bring you down," declares the Lord (Obadiah 1:2-4).

Remember, Satan was cast out from heaven by God due to his pride that led him to rebel against Yahweh. When Lucifer stood next to God, His light would shine upon Lucifer's jewels placed upon him by God. It was *God's* beauty reflecting off the jewels set on Lucifer making him appear beautiful. Lucifer's beauty was not his own. In like fashion, any beauty you or I may possess, it is not ours. We have nothing of our own to be prideful. Lucifer became blinded by the brilliant light reflecting off him. His wisdom became corrupt and ineffective, causing him to determine more extraordinary things about himself than reality.

Everyone wants to be God or like God and to have all His power, but *few* want to be like Jesus, *lowly and humble.* Jesus is the only connection humans have to God the Father, His Kingdom, and His glory. To quote David E. Taylor once more from his book, *Victory Over Pride,* "*One can never crush an invisible enemy; neither can we crush him if we do not know he is attacking. Satan has strategically tricked mankind into attributing many behavioral patterns in our lives to reasons other than what is true. It is pride that hinders us from seeking the Lord and praying, hence causing us to walk in discord with others…pride also hinders us from receiving correction, blessings, reproof, instruction, wisdom, knowledge, and the fullness of God. It is pride that hinders people from looking at others the way Jesus does, which is with a single eye. Pride binds and blinds. A sign of a mature Christian can humbly receive correction or rebuke, deserved or undeserved.*"

> "And so all Israel will be saved, as it is written: 'The deliverer will come from Zion; He will turn godlessness away from Jacob. And this is My covenant with them when I take away their sins (Romans 11:26-27).'"

If there is a way into a situation, there is a way out. No matter our weaknesses, if we are humble enough to deal with them through Holy Spirit, when the weaknesses arise, we will grow stronger in Christ instead of weaker. This is what is meant in II Peter 3:18, "*grow in grace.*" The Father can exalt us as we walk humbly. Many ministries

have fallen from the place God ordained because of division and strife caused by pride. We would all get further in life, relationships, businesses, ministry, etc., if we humbled ourselves to walk like Jesus and approach situations as He.

"God has exalted Jesus and gave Him a name above all names," reads Philippians 2:9. We are to make ourselves of no reputation, of no account. Watchman Nee is quoted as having said in *Watchman Nee: Sufferer for China,* "The lower we put something, the safer it is. It is safest to put a cap on the floor, meaning that the more a Christian is humbled, the safer it is for him. In fact, the safest place this side of heaven is the cross."

We must to allow God to make our name great versus trying with futility to do it ourselves. If we humble our name, He will make it great. If we exalt our own name, He cannot. Jesus never got into arguments, contentions, or disagreements with people or even with His enemies. He retained peace that surpassed all understanding and knowledge (Philippians 4:7). He has left us that same peace; we need simply to choose to keep it.

Notes

Chapter 8

Fear of the Lord

"The fear of the Lord teaches a man wisdom, and humility comes before honor (Proverbs 15:33)."

"Better to be lowly in spirit and among the oppressed than to share plunder with the proud (Proverbs 16:19)."

Just as pride comes before the fall, humility comes before honor—there is no honor without humility first. A humble person demands to be judged and reckoned by others. A pious person may find little difficulty humbling himself to God, but balks at correction from superiors, equals, or inferiors. We need to be exceedingly cautious of *"prideful humility"* [false humility].

If *outward* humility is not the result of *inward* humility, it is dangerous because it becomes an outward deception. To put it another way, the outward expression of humility must always result from inward grace at work. Humility is the direct nature of God. Take advantage of every opportunity to be humble.

Jesus is humility personified. We all know that if we are accused of something for which we are guilty, we must confess, apologize and make it right. However, what if we are wrongfully accused? What then? Do we have the right to jump into a debate with someone, declaring how wrong they are about us? Absolutely not. Instead of arguing, respond by apologizing to them for having given them the impression we did or said what they perceive we did or said. Ask how to make it right. How can they come against us in the face of humility? For example, if someone says in a gruff tone, *"You did this all wrong! What were you thinking?"* We can respond humbly with, *"I apologize. I can see how I could have done that better. Can you advise me of a better way so next time I'll do better?"*

We need to get it burrowed into our spirit-man that our defender [Christ] is far greater than the offender [Satan]. We are never to be defensive. Walk away if we must, but don't get into a showdown of words trying to convince someone they are wrong; when has that ever accomplished anything good? When someone is convinced of an untruth, no amount of arguing can divert them. Only God can change a heart. Don't waste time and energy. We should never jeopardize our personal walk with God because of false accusations. It isn't worth it. God will prove them wrong in time; we needn't concern ourselves with such petty matters. The truth will always surface in due season. Keep integrity intact and it will protect us in the long run.

Agree Quickly:

"Agree quickly with your adversary (Matthew 5:25)."

"It is already a defeat for you, that you have lawsuits with one another. Why not rather be wronged? Why not rather be defrauded (II Corinthians 6:7)."

"We are to clothe ourselves daily in humility (I Peter 5:5)."

A prideful person thinks only of their rights. A humble person thinks only of what is right. We are thinking only of ourselves when we are more concerned about being wronged than what Yahweh wants us to learn or see in a situation. Let God produce His perfect work of patience and love. Daily we must ask God to strip us of any and all pride, bathe us in righteousness, and clothe us in humility. Ask God to help stir faith deeply within. The stronger the faith, the closer the walk, the easier to recognize pride, the faster we can allow Him to help remove it and replace it with humility, the more we are as Jesus.

This is where pulling down strongholds and imaginations (II Corinthians 10:3-6) enters, *"For though we live in this world, we do not wage war as the world does. The weapons we fight with are not the weapons of the world. On the contrary, they have divine power to demolish strongholds. We demolish arguments and every pretension that sets itself up against the knowledge of God, and we take captive every thought to make it obedient to Christ. And we will be ready to punish every act of disobedience once your obedience is complete."*

When our thoughts become prideful thinking more highly of ourselves than we ought, take the authority Jesus Christ has given and pull those thoughts down and out. This text is written because God understands the frail condition of the flesh. Don't allow pride to fester and manifest. Pride is foolishness on any level. Be ready to punish all disobedience in life.

Pray for Holy Spirit to stir discernment. Anyone in whom Holy Spirit dwells, discernment is present. Remember, there is a difference between *discernment* and *prejudice*, between *righteous judgment* and being *judgmental*. Surrender to the call of humility confessing daily to Yahweh that you *choose* to walk humbly in all your ways. Command the spirits of pride and rebellion to depart from your midst replacing them with humility and obedience. Holy Spirit within is the only One who has the power to overcome pride. Allow Him to guide you into holiness, humility, and compliance.

Prayer:

O Father God, in heaven, hallowed be Thy name in all the Earth. I desire with all my spirit, heart, soul, and body to be humble as Christ Himself was humble as He walked the Earth. Show me the difference between timidity and humility; discernment and being judgmental. I thank You for giving me a new heart and new spirit. Lay Your heart of humility, grace, mercy, and compassion within me so that I never stray from truth. Show me how to be obedient as You see obedience, Jesus. I love You. Show me how to never forsake You as You never forsake me.

Note

Chapter 9

Spirit, Water, and Blood

Water Scriptures:

Now on the last day, the great day of the feast, Jesus stood and cried out, saying, "If anyone is thirsty, let him come to Me and drink. The one who believes in Me, as the Scripture said, 'From his innermost being will flow rivers of living water.'" But this He said in reference to the Spirit, whom those who believed in Him were to receive…(John 7:37-39).

"Jesus answered and said to her, 'Everyone who drinks of this water will be thirsty again; but whoever drinks of the water that I will give him shall never be thirsty; but the water that I will give him will become in him a fountain of water springing up to eternal life (John 4:13-14)."

"Lord, the hope of Israel, all who abandon You will be put to shame. Those who turn away on earth will be written down, because they have forsaken the fountain of living water, that is the Lord (Jeremiah 17:13)."

"And on that day living waters will flow out of Jerusalem…in summer as well as in winter. And the Lord will be King over all the earth; on that day the Lord will be the only one, and His name the only one (Zechariah 14:8-9)."

"Then He said to me, 'It is done.' I am the Alpha and the Omega, the beginning and the end. I will give water to the one who thirsts from the spring of the water of life, without cost (Revelations 21:6)."

The Water, the Spirit, and the Blood Scriptures:

This is the One who came by water and blood, Jesus Christ; not with the water only, but with the water and with the blood. It is the Spirit who testifies, because the Spirit is the truth. For there are three that testify: the Spirit and the water and the blood; and the three are in agreement (I John 5:6-8).

"…pierced His side…immediately blood and water came out (John 19:34)."

"Corresponding to that, baptism now saves you—not the removal of dirt from the flesh, but an appeal to God for a good conscience…(I Peter 3:20-21)."

The Water and the Spirit Scriptures:

Then I will sprinkle clean water on you, and you will be clean; I will cleanse you from all your filthiness and from all your idols. Moreover, I will give you a new heart and put a new spirit within you; and I will remove the heart of stone from your flesh and give you a heart of flesh. And I will put My Spirit within you and bring it about that you walk in My statutes, and are careful and follow My ordinances (Ezekiel 36:25-27).

"For I will pour water on the thirsty land and streams on the dry ground; I will pure out My Spirit on your offspring, and My blessing on your descendants (Isaiah 44:3)."

"And he showed me a river of the water of life, clear as crystal, coming from the throne of God and of the Lamb...the Spirit and the bride say, 'Come.' And let the one who hears say, 'Come.' And let the one who is thirsty come; let the one who desires, take the water of life without cost (Revelation 22:1, 17)."

"For by one Spirit we were all baptized into one body...we were all made to drink of one Spirit (I Corinthians 12:13)."

"For John baptized with water, but you will be baptized with the Holy Spirit not many days from now (Acts 1:5)."

Born of Water and the Spirit:

> "…unless one is born of water and the Spirit he cannot enter into the kingdom of God. That which is born of the flesh is flesh, and that which is born of the Spirit is spirit (John 3:5-6)."

*A*s you can see by these few Scriptures—and there are so many more, living water is mentioned from Genesis to Revelation. I used to see, *"Come to Me and drink,"* as taking something from Christ like a child would take water from a parent—the water is external. Upon further review, I now understand that the *"Living Water"* is Christ. We're not taking something [water] from Christ; we're taking Christ [the Living Water]. Since the Father, Son, and Holy Spirit are one, the water is also the Spirit.

A big question on believer's minds is, *"What does it mean to be born of water, blood, and the Spirit?"* In the garden, a guard struck Jesus' side. Water and blood spilled. The water is the representation of the pure, cleansing water of the Word [The Living Water], which is Christ and the Spirit. Water ran from Jesus because He is water. The *water* [spiritually] washes over and through the one who comes to Christ. It purifies and washes the sin nature as a whole. Once cleansed, *Holy Spirit* is allowed to move in making our inner-man His dwelling place. Jesus [The Water] grants mankind access to the Spirit.

The blood sealant then covers completely the new sinless being who is filled with Christ. Simply stated, we are washed with the *water of the Word*, God's *Spirit* is deposited, and then Christ is sealed in us by the holy *blood*. The Spirit cannot be removed by any act of sin.

Only blaspheming Holy Spirit can one lose the Spirit, and that would be a permanent removal. We will discuss this in-depth later.

It is God's Spirit uniting the Body of Christ. We "*drink of one Spirit*," therefore we all drink of the same water and eat of the same body. To *drink* His water is humbling ourselves recognizing our sinfulness and our need for cleansing that only Christ can provide. Receiving the pure water is the entrance, and then the blood can seal. The passage in John 19 also shows that the blood and water are merged—they work together. Supernaturally, blood came from Jesus' pores where there naturally would have been only water.

The "*baptism*" [immersion] of His holy water is what merges us into Yahweh. *First* the baptism and *then* salvation. Many get it backwards. I have always heard, "*Get saved, then get baptized.*" Mark 16:16 reads, "*He who has believed and has been baptized shall be saved, but he who has disbelieved shall be condemned.*" The one who has been baptized in the Spirit through belief—afterward and because of—shall be saved. This depicts spiritual emersion into Christ. It gives the sense of being cleansed internally by the water of the Word allowing one to be overtaken by the Spirit of God.

To reiterate, the water purifies the new home for the Spirit to safely dwell, thereby allowing the Spirit to take residence. The Spirit brings the blood covering. The blood sealant protects Holy Spirit, as well as the believer, from becoming impure. The only way to remove the water, Spirit, and blood is to completely turn our backs against God, as did Lucifer. Our spirit cannot otherwise be tarnished by sin.

Being consumed by the pure water grants the confidence to enter the holy place since only the holy can enter. It is Christ's holiness through us that we can obtain such privilege. King David compares a close walk with the Lord as a mighty tree planted in the steams of waters (Psalm 1). When we are consumed by Holy Spirit, we will be overtaken with the Word of God, and we will delight in it. To delight in the Word makes one unshakable. To be planted by the *"streams of water"* refers to the Living Water [Christ].

Clean Feet:

"… that He might sanctify her, having cleansed her by the washing of water by the word, that He might present to Himself the church in all her glory, having no spot or wrinkle or any such thing; but that she would be holy and blameless (Ephesians 5:26-27)."

"He who believes in Me, as the Scripture said, 'From his innermost being will flow rivers of living water' (John 7:38).'"

"Then he showed me a river of the water of life, clear as crystal, coming from the throne of God and of the Lamb…and let the one who is thirsty come; let the one who wishes take the water of life without cost (Revelation 22:1, 17)."

He…began to wash the disciples' feet and to wipe them with the towel…Simon Peter said to Him, "Lord, do You wash my feet?" Jesus answered and said to him, "What I do you do not realize now, but you will understand hereafter." Peter said to Him, "Never shall You wash my feet." Jesus answered him, "If I do not wash you, you have no part with Me." Simon

Peter said to Him, "Lord, then wash not only my feet, but also my hands and my head." Jesus said to him, "He who has bathed needs only to wash his feet, but is completely clean… (John 13:5-14).

"How will they preach unless they are sent? Just as it is written, 'How beautiful are the feet of those who bring good news of good things' (Romans 10:15)."

Once we receive the water, Holy Spirit is automatically ushered into us. Jesus was prepared to wash Peter's feet when Peter told Him, "*No.*" Jesus insisted, and Peter responded asking Jesus to wash his whole body! This is understandable from a human standpoint, but what Peter did not comprehend is that our feet touch the Earth. If a person's feet are cleansed, his whole body is kept from the impurities of the world. This translates into the spiritual by realizing that man's feet are what touch the Earth—they are our connection to the world. The feet represent that which can cause one to be tainted by the world and its lusts or that which can keep us purified, orderly, and righteous.

Jesus washing Peter's physical feet represents how Jesus' holy water washes the dirtiest part of man connecting us to the world [lusts of the flesh], which is our soul. The soul [mind, will, and emotions] must come under subjection to the Spirit of God. When His holy water washes through our soul, the Spirit merges with our spirit. This way, the Spirit via our spirit instructs the clean soul what to do and the body follows suit. Whatever the soul instructs, the body does. The spirit relates to God, the soul relates to self, and the body relates to the world. Since the soul relates to self and we're instructed to die to self, the water cleanses [baptized the flesh into Jesus' death] that which controls the body so that it isn't allowed to wrongly connect to the condemned world.

James 1:27 states that true religion is keeping oneself unstained by the world. This can only happen by regularly washing with the purity of Christ. If we keep our feet [soul] continually cleansed, the outward man will stay clean. In Romans 10, the feet bringing good news are called "*beautiful.*" When a person's feet usher something, the whole body comes along. Clean feet—the good news of good things. Dirty feet—bad news of bad things from the tainting of this dark and dying world.

For instance, if one is covered in mud tracking the floor, the whole house is considered dirty. Their feet tracked the mud. However, if they are covered in mud but remove the dirty shoes and walk into the house with clean, bare feet, they can manage to get to the shower without muddying anything. It is the feet that touch the floor, not the rest of their body. We can manage to keep our arms up, keeping them from touching anything. The cleanliness of our feet determines the cleanliness of our surroundings.

Notice Jesus knew who would betray Him, yet He still washed the feet of all the disciples. He did not exclude Judas. This says that many who *outwardly* proclaim Jesus Christ do not indeed receive Him *inwardly*. These people have had the water poured over them but do not allow it to penetrate their spirit and soul. Hence, these people are not truly cleansed and have no part in Christ. This is a warning to seek Him intimately allowing Him to show any and every wicked way hidden inside. All who say, "*Lord, Lord,*" are not His own.

Notes

Chapter 10

~Blood is Life

Blood for Blood:

Surely I will require your lifeblood; from every beast I will require it. And from every man, from every man's brother I will require the life of man. For whoever sheds man's blood, by man his blood shall be shed. For in the image of God He made man (Genesis 9:4-6).

"For He who requires blood remembers them; He does not forget the cry of the afflicted (Psalm 9:12)."

"He will rescue their life from oppression and violence, and their blood will be precious in His sight (Psalm 72:14)."

"Why should the nations say, 'Where is their God?' Let there be known among the nations in our sight, vengeance for the blood of Your servants which has been shed (Psalm 79:10)."

"I will avenge their blood which I have not avenged, for the Lord swells in Zion (Joel 3:21)."

"*O*nly *you shall not eat the blood; you are to pour it out on the ground like water…be sure not to eat the blood, for the blood is the life, and you shall not eat the life with the flesh,*" states Deuteronomy 12:16 and 23. Simply stated, blood is the physical body's life. To consume the blood of anything is to defile its life. God deems blood sacred because He devised a blood system for the atonement of sin. Blood is a symbol of life. It is given for the life of another when making satisfaction for wrongdoing. This is why the sacrificed animal had to be pure. Its lifeblood indicated purity. The blood's purity covered the impurity of sin.

Leviticus 17:10-12 also reads, "*And any man…who eats any blood, I will set My face against that person who eats blood and will cut him off from among his people. For the life of the flesh is in the blood, and I have given it to you on the altar to make atonement for your souls; for it is the blood because of the life that makes atonement.*" This is why mankind must receive a blood transfusion from the heavenly realm. The physical life of the flesh is its blood. We come into the world of our earthly parents, one sin generation after another, with the tainted blood of Adam. When we consign our sin-nature to God [the natural bloodline], we can receive in its place the blood of the flesh of Christ [the sinless One].

God became man [Jesus], and man killed Him. The repercussion is that every man's blood is required as penance for the blood of Jesus. This is where, spiritually speaking, we must "*die to the flesh,*" as I keep repeating. To become truly born-again, death is required. We give up our earthly blood by dying—spiritually speaking—becoming re-born, taking on the untainted blood of Jesus Christ. This is a required blood transfusion. In the natural, when a person undergoes a transfusion, their body raises up from the hospital bed looking exactly the same outwardly, but their life source is now completely different.

Blood is everything to God because it is the essence of the life He gave to man and beast. In the Old Testament, they were to respect and be careful with the blood of anything living. It is a respect for the lives sacrificed for the life of another. Blood is so precious to the Father that, though many servants of God have had their blood shed for Him even unto death, He will take vengeance upon their slayers. God rescues the afflicted. No drop of blood of His ambassadors goes unnoticed because it is God's blood running through our veins.

Ezekiel 35:6 reads, *"Therefore as I live,"* declares the Lord God, *"I will give you over to bloodshed, and bloodshed will pursue you; since you have not hated bloodshed, therefore bloodshed will pursue you."* Jeremiah 46:10 also states, *"For that day belongs to the Lord God of hosts, a day of vengeance, to avenge Himself on His foes; and the sword will devour, and it shall be covered and made drunk with their blood; for there will be a slaughter for the Lord God of hosts..."*

The sword of the Lord is filled with the blood of those who have not obeyed and slaughtered His valued bondservants. The Lord's wrath is without measure against those who have set themselves against Him. To go against one of God's people is to go against God personally.

"You shall not eat anything with the blood, nor practice divination or soothsaying (Leviticus 19:26)."

The people rushed greedily upon the spoil, and took sheep and oxen and calves, and slew them on the ground; and the people ate them with the blood. Then they told Saul, saying, "Behold, the people are sinning against the Lord by eating with the blood." And he said, "You have acted treacherously; roll a great stone to me today." Saul said, "Disperse yourselves among the people and say to them, 'Each one of you bring me his ox or his sheep, and slaughter it here and eat; and do not sin against the Lord by eating with the blood (I Samuel 14:32-34)."

This last Scripture in I Samuel 14 calls eating of the blood *"treacherous"* and a sin against God. The greedy in life, especially today, have no consciousness of the value of blood—life. The greedy forget the ways of God; they eat blood. In other words, they take the lives of others literally, metaphorically, mentally, emotionally, and spiritually. When we understand that blood represents life, we will take much more care how we treat others. Shedding of blood today is spiritual as well as physical. We slaughter people with words of hatred, prejudice, malice, greed, slander, gossip, blasphemy, and anything else against God. It happens within the church. The church should be united as one, not divided one against the other.

Notes

Chapter 11

Value of the Fat

"...the head and the fat...on the fire that is on the altar" (Leviticus 1:8, 12).

"It is a perpetual statute...you shall not eat any fat or any blood (Leviticus 3:17)."

"You shall not eat any manner of fat...his own hands are to bring offerings by fire to the Lord. He shall bring the fat...the priest shall offer up the fat in smoke on the altar...the one... who offers the blood of the peace offerings and the fat, the right thigh shall be his as his portion(Leviticus 7:23, 30-33).

"...offer up the fat in smoke as a soothing aroma to the Lord (Leviticus 17:6)."

Sacred Fat:

*A*s is the blood, the *fat* of a sacrifice is sacred to God. Fat keeps things tender from becoming rigid and inflexible. The oil [grease] from the fat keeps things lubricated. Fat is a protective covering for the blood, bones, and all innards of a being. A cooked meat with no fat isn't nearly as tender, tasty, or juicy as a piece of meat with fat. Fat stirs the juices enhancing the taste. It even has a pleasing aroma while cooking. Fat begins like water but becomes thickened like a salve.

Generally speaking, no one wants a starving animal because they're too bony and unsightly. Fat, when balanced, is an excellent thing. It is a mark of wealth and prosperity, whereas lean signifies poverty and lack. Have you ever heard a larger person comment that, if they should fall, they have plenty of cushioning to break their fall? Skinny, scrawny, people snap like twigs.

When we flip that concept into the spiritual, fat keeps the lifeblood from curdling and becoming dry and brittle. It protects a person's heart from brittleness. It keeps a person *"juicy and tender,"* even tasty with a sweet aroma unto the Father. Again, in essence, the fat is a tenderizing protective covering to the blood crucial to the life of a being.

We are to be fat in the Word of God. It is likened unto being fattened by Holy Spirit working in our lives. The fatter we are in Holy Spirit, the more we are protected from being crushed by the enemy. When we are lean in Holy Spirit, we are left as open prey for the devil. The more stout spiritually, the thicker and stronger we become in Christ.

In the Old Testament, the fat always had to be burned with fire, sent to heaven in smoke. In the smoke, a sweet aroma was received by God from the person offering the sacrifice. We, the believer, must be burned by holy fire in the spiritual sense. When we allow the fleshly nature to be burned by the fire of His Word, the fat [the good stuff] becomes sweet and fragrant to the Yahweh. He smells our tenderness toward Him.

Blessing of Fat:

"For we are a fragrance of Christ to God…(II Corinthians 2:15)."

"and walk in love, just as Christ also loved you and gave Himself up for us, an offering and a sacrifice to God as a fragrant aroma (Ephesians 5:2)."

As for the portions of fat…and he offered them up in smoke on the altar…Moses and Aaron went into the tent of meeting. When they came out and blessed the people, the glory of the Lord appeared to all the people. Then fire came out from before the Lord and consumed the burnt offering and the portions of fat on the altar; and when all the people saw it, they shouted and fell on their faces (Leviticus 9:19-20, 23-24).

"The sword of the Lord is filled with blood, it is covered with fat, with the blood of lambs and goats, with the fat of the kidneys of rams. For the Lord has a sacrifice in Bozrah and a great slaughter in the land of Edom (Isaiah 34:6)."

Leviticus 1:8 & 12 puts the fat with the head to be burned. The head is our thinking—the mind of Christ. He is our head. Spiritual *"fatness"* protects our minds from Satan. This fatness represents the fullness of the Spirit of God, not gluttony. If we are lean in the Spirit of God, our head is open to all sorts of worldly thoughts. The blood, the fat, and the Spirit work together. In Leviticus 9 above, the burning of the fat directly correlates to people being blessed by God able to manifest Himself to all the people.

When the Lord justifies taking vengeance upon those who have slaughtered His people, He then makes His sword complete with the life [fat and blood] of His enemies. God is chastising His people for not filling Him with the fat of their sacrifices. Again, it is considered a great sin to not lift the fat of an offering, meaning they were not desirous of giving Him the best, their all.

Proverbs 28:25 reads, "*He that is of a proud heart stirs up strife, but he that puts his trust in the Lord shall be made fat.*" Notice in these verses that the fat is used in a positive context. The diligent is made "fat;" good news, which comes from God, puts "*fat on the bones*," and trust in the Lord makes one fat. We must desire to be fattened by the Spirit of the Lord so that the fullness of life can be experienced as God's kings and priests. Holy Spirit is the fat. He keeps us tenderized with an obedient, loving heart toward the Lord.

"You have brought Me not sweet cane with honey, nor have you filled Me with the fat of your sacrifices; rather you have burdened Me with your sins, you have wearied Me with your iniquities (Isaiah 43:24)."

"And the Lord shall guide you continually, and satisfy your soul in drought, and make fat your bones; and you shall be like a watered garden, and like a spring of water, whose waters fail not (Isaiah 58:11)."

"The word of the Lord came...you eat the fat and clothe yourselves with the wool, you slaughter the fat sheep without feeding the flock (Ezekiel 34:3)."

"...but the soul of the diligent is made fat (Proverbs 13:4)."
"...good news puts fat on the bones (Proverbs 15:30)."

The Passover:

"The priest shall take some of the blood from the sin offering and put it on the door posts of the house, on the four corners of the ledge of the altar and on the posts of the gate of the inner court (Ezekiel 45:19)."

Your lamb shall be an unblemished male a year old...then the whole assembly of the congregation of Israel is to kill it at twilight. Moreover, they shall take some of the blood and put it on the two doorposts and on the lintel of the houses in which they eat it. They shall eat the flesh that same night, roasted with fire, and they shall eat it with unleavened bread and bitter herbs. Do not eat any of it raw or boiled at all with water, but rather roasted with fire…and you shall not leave any of it over until morning, but whatever is left of it until morning, you shall burn with fire. Now you shall eat it in this manner: with your loins girded, your sandals on your feet, and your staff in your hand; and you shall eat it in haste – it is the Lord's Passover. For I will go through the land of Egypt on that night, and will strike down all the firstborn in the land of Egypt I will execute judgments – I am the Lord. The blood shall be a sign for you on the houses where you live; and when I see the blood I will pass over you, and no plague will befall you to destroy you when I strike the land of Egypt (Exodus 12:5-13).

"Being justified as a gift by His grace through the redemption which is in Christ Jesus; whom God displayed publicly as a propitiation in His blood through faith. This was to demonstrate His righteousness, because in the forbearance of God He passed over the sins previously committed (Romans 3:24-25)."

These are very common passages, yet so much is missed. This is a foreshadowing of events to come:

First, to put the blood over the doorposts and lintels represents being covered in the spirit realm by the blood of the pure Lamb in the New Testament.

Second, it states they were to "*eat the flesh the same night*" and "eat it in haste." This is a depiction of consuming the Word of God without hesitation. There is very little time, in the grand scheme of things, which is why it states, "*with your loins girded, your sandals on your feet, and your staff in your hand.*" Be prepared, alert, and on the watch, for He comes like a thief in the night.

Third, it is to be "*roasted with fire…eaten with unleavened bread and bitter herbs.*" God is the all-consuming fire. Holy fire brings purification. Unleavened bread represents untainted [pure]. Bitter herbs mean the bitterness of the cost of the cross, the pain, and suffering that comes with sacrificing our fleshly nature.

Fourth, the blood as a sign signifies the pure blood of Christ poured over each of us. Blood is the life of a being. Here, the Lamb had to be without blemish, pure, just as Jesus is the pure, unblemished Lamb of God. As the blood was put over the doors and lintels, it must be "*placed over*" the doors of our hearts and spirit man, our inner being.

Personal Responsibility for the Blood of Others:

God repeatedly warns before He drops His wrath on the disobedient. Our responsibility is to lead the wayward to repentance. If we neglect our duty, they will die in their sin and rendering their blood as penance. Blood is also required of those who failed to inform the wicked to turn them from their sin. What more can I add to these Scriptures to make it more clear?

> Then he who hears the sound of the trumpet and does not take warning, and a sword comes and takes him away, his blood will be on his own head. He heard the sound of the trumpet but did not take warning; his blood will be on himself. But had he taken warning, he would have delivered his life. But if the watchman sees the sword coming and does not blow the trumpet and the people are not warned, and a sword comes and takes a person from them, he is taken away in his iniquity; but his blood I will require from the watchman's hand.' Now as for you, son of man, I have appointed you a watchman for the house of Israel; so you will hear a message from My mouth and give them warning from Me. When I say to the wicked, 'O wicked man, you will surely die,' and you do not speak to warn the wicked from his way, that wicked man shall die in his iniquity, but his blood I will require from your hand. But if you on your part warn a wicked man to turn from his way, he will die in his iniquity, but you have delivered your life (Ezekiel 33:4-8).

> Therefore, I testify to you this day that I am innocent of the blood of all men. For I did not shrink from declaring to you the whole purpose of God. Be on guard for yourselves and for all the flock, among which the Holy Spirit has made you overseers, to shepherd the church of God which He purchased with His own blood (Acts 20:26-28).

Matthew 27:4 & 6 read, "[*Judas*]...*I have sinned by betraying innocent blood...the chief priests took the pieces of silver and said, 'It is not lawful to put them into the temple treasury since it is the price of blood.*'" Even the priests who paid Judas to betray Jesus, when Judas returned the silver to them, would not put the money they gave him back into the treasury. Though they were men who did not walk in obedience to God, they still understood the basic principle of blood—blood money—and its value and power.

One of the reasons the Israelites have had so many problems throughout the ages is their willingness to take on the blood of Jesus when Pilate washed his hands of it. Wanting to crucify Jesus, they cried, *"His blood shall be on our children and us."* They cursed themselves and their generations to come. This wasn't the blood of just any man, but the God-Man. This was their greatest act of rebellion against God.

God Became Man:

"Come now, and let us reason together," says the Lord, "Though your sins are as scarlet, they will be as white as snow; though they are red like crimson, they will be like wool (Isaiah 1:18)."

"Therefore since the children share in flesh and blood, He Himself likewise also partook of the same [flesh and blood], that through death He might render powerless him who had the power of death, that is, the devil," reads Hebrews 2:14. His love for you and me is so immeasurable that He took our blood and flesh. Although He was all God, He was also all man,

suffering as we suffer in the body. He took into Himself the "*red blood*" of mankind and replaced it with His own pure white blood. Translation: the sin-drenched stain of mankind was removed for all who receive His blood atonement.

Notes

hearts filled with /Gratitude —

the word,
your love + forgiveness
our many many blessings
that we take for
grant

Chapter 12

~Blood Covenant

Jesus…said, "Take, eat; this is My body…drink from it, all of you; for this is My blood of the covenant, which is poured out for many for forgiveness of sins (Matthew 26:26-28).

"…This cup is the new covenant in My blood; do this, as often as you drink it, in remembrance of Me (I Corinthians 11:27)."

With the New Covenant, we are now to eat the fat and drink the blood. Animals who were sacrificed did not willingly give their lives; they were taken by their owner. The sacrificed animal was holy in the sight of God, and its life was to be honored. Its blood and fat were not to be defiled.

In the case of Jesus, He willingly gave His life's blood and body for our atonement which changes everything. Now it is required to eat the fat and drink the blood to take the sacrificed life. In eating the body and drinking the blood of a being, we take on its life's essence. To eat something is to become one with it because it is consumed

Learn

merging with our whole being. To eat of and drink *in* Jesus Christ, spiritually speaking, we become one with Him.

As God became man sharing in our flesh and blood, in turn, we are to share in His flesh and blood. He became *like* us—we are to become *as* He. Since He died in the flesh, we also need to die to our fleshly nature, follow in His steps, and live unto Him in His resurrection.

> And, thou son of man, thus says the Lord God, "Speak unto every kind of bird and to every beast of the field, 'Assemble and come, gather from every side to My sacrifice on the mountains of Israel, that you may eat flesh and drink blood. You shall eat the flesh of the mighty, and drink the blood of the princes of the Earth, of rams, of lambs, and of goats, of bullocks, all of the fatlings of Bashan. So you will eat fat until you are glutted, and drink blood until you are drunk, from My sacrifice which I have sacrificed for you. You will be glutted at My table with horses and charioteers, with mighty men and all the men of war," declares the Lord God. "And I will set My glory among the nations; and all the nations will see My judgment which I have executed and My hand which I have laid on them. And the house of Israel will know that I am the Lord their God from that day on (Ezekiel 39:17-21).

Read

> So Jesus said to them, "Truly, truly, I say to you, unless you eat the flesh of the Son of Man and drink His blood, you have no life in yourselves. He who eats My flesh and drinks My blood has eternal life, and I will raise him up on the last

day. For My flesh is true food, and My blood is true drink. He who eats My flesh and drinks My blood abides in Me, and I in him (John 6:53-56)."

In this text, God speaks of being glutted [stuffed] at His table, eating the fat, and drinking the blood of mighty men and princes of the Earth. This is God's vengeance upon those who slew His people. By consuming their fat and blood, God's people become the mighty and the princes. God's power, authority, and glory will then shine mightily for the entire world to know that God is the overcoming God.

Eternal life can come only through consuming the flesh and blood of Christ. The way to *"consume"* the Word is to willingly lay aside self so that when we read or hear God's Word, we purpose to receive revelation, not just information. The Church needs to correct her way of thinking. Raised in Church, I often heard, *"Jesus is in my heart,"* which is based on II Corinthians 1:22 stating, *"…the Spirit in our hearts."* That sounds holy and scriptural, but it is a misconception. What I hear from that statement is, *"I am still me in my body, but Jesus resides in a small section of me, separate from the rest of my body."* This mindset is still separation from God—two beings dwelling in one place. It's roommates versus marriage. II Corinthians 1 references the overtaking of a person's heart, as in an exchange of our heart for His, not a little Jesus in a little compartment of our heart.

Our new way of thinking as a believer should be, *"All of me is given over to all of Him. He does not 'live in my heart,' but rather, 'His heart has consumed me, and He is my heartbeat.'"* In light of that, our entire being is now merged with His. His Spirit is in us and communes with our spirit. Because we died to our fleshly nature, the only nature now in operation is His. This is why so many do not have intimacy with Christ; they only talk about *"Jesus saves."* They cannot hear from Him like friends speak because they are not really friends. If Jesus just lives *in* their heart, they are not unified simply standing nearby. It is the difference between a close acquaintance and becoming one being, as in marriage.

Understand clearly that, when we are merged with Jesus Christ, His voice is inwardly audible. Before His death, burial and resurrection, His voice was outwardly audible because His Spirit had not been inserted into the majority of His people. Think of it as an empty canister with a voice recorder dropped in and playing from *within*. The voice was once heard from *without* the canister, but now from *within*. God was on the outside of His people, but He is now on the inside through Holy Spirit deposit.

Intimacy and our ever-growing relationship with Him allow us to know the difference between His voice, the voice of Satan, or our own nonsensical head voice. Just as I know the voices of my earthly husband and father, more so, I know well the voice of my heavenly Husband and Father. It is distinct and sure. It is more apparent today than last year or a few days ago. The more we hear His voice, the more familiar it becomes.

Redemption – Eternal Covenant

"So Moses took the blood and sprinkled it on the people, and said, 'Behold the blood of the covenant...(Exodus 24:8).'"

"Much more then, having now been justified by His blood, we shall be saved from the wrath of God through Him (Romans 5:9)."

"In whom we have redemption through His blood, even the forgiveness of sins…and through Him to reconcile all things to Himself, having made peace through the blood of His cross; through Him, I say, whether things on Earth or things in heaven (Colossians 1:14, 20)."

If you address as Father the One who impartially judges according to each one's work, conduct yourselves in fear during the time of your stay on Earth; knowing that you were not redeemed with perishable things…but with precious blood, as of a lamb unblemished and spotless, the blood of Christ (I Peter 1:17-19).

The covenant God made with Moses was temporary. The new covenant is everlasting, sealed by the blood of the holy Lamb of God. He shed His blood [life], so to cover all who will receive. His life was given on the cross, but the blood is the essence of life. When He rose from the dead, it proved that His blood is eternal and cannot be destroyed. When we are washed with the pure water, filled with Holy Spirit, and covered by His eternal blood, we become transformed into an eternal being like Christ. This is the regeneration: we die to one bloodline [earthly] and live through another [heavenly].

Through the gift of His blood, a people who were once far off can now draw near (Ephesians 2:13). It is by His blood in us that we can draw near to the perfect, pure, and holy God.

"I will remove their blood from their mouth and their detestable things from between their teeth. Then they also will be a remnant for our God…as for you also, because of the blood of My covenant with you, I have set your prisoners free from the waterless pit (Zechariah 9:7, 11)."

Notes

Chapter 13 NIV:

Aliens and Strangers

Strangers
+ pilgrams

Heavenly Origin:

"Beloved, I urge you as aliens and strangers to abstain from fleshly lusts which wage war against the soul. Keep your behavior excellent…(I Peter 2:11)." NIV

For He Himself is our peace, who made both groups into one and broke down the barrier of the dividing wall, by abolishing in His flesh the enmity, which is the Law of commandments contained in ordinances, so that in Himself He might make the two into one new man, thus establishing peace, and might reconcile them both in one body to God through the cross, by it having put to death the enmity. And He came and preached peace to you who were far away, and peace to those who were near; for through Him we both have our access in one Spirit to the Father (Ephesians 2:14-18).

*T*his concept is so complicated for the average person to understand because it is far and away from the trappings of religiosity and world view. To recap, our origin at birth from our earthly father and mother is *"of the Earth."* When we choose the blood of Jesus, we relinquish the earthly origin. This means we put away [die to] the ways of the world. When we take up that death, like Jesus, then, and only then, can we receive a new life through a new birth. By accepting the blood covenant through rebirth, our origin literally changes. Now we are born *"of heaven."* Being born of heaven, we take Jesus Christ with all His supernatural abilities and attributes.

This is why, in John 14:12, Jesus told the disciples not to be sad about Him leaving because, with the anointing of His Spirit, we will do greater things than He. His Spirit [essence], is inserted within us. We need to stop thinking of Jesus as being *"in our heart"* and start believing that we are one being with Him through faith. He is now our very heart, the life of our existence.

Peter refers to those in Christ as *"aliens and strangers."* Why? It is because our origin has changed from the earthly to the heavenly. When the earthly nature was put to death, death stopped the effects of that nature. We were regenerated from death into a new life through the water, Spirit, and blood of Christ who is of heaven. If we now originate from heaven, the Earth is not our home making us aliens on this planet. Note I Peter 2:11 above.

Ezekiel 16:1-6 astounds me. It reads, *"Then the word of the Lord came to me, saying, 'Son of man, make known to Jerusalem her abominations and say, "Thus says the Lord God to Jerusalem, 'Your origin and your birth are from the land of the Canaanite, your father was an Amorite and your mother, a Hittite. As for your birth, on the day you were born, your navel cord was not cut, nor were you washed with water for cleansing; you were not rubbed with salt or even wrapped in cloths. No eye looked with pity on you to do any of these things for you, to have compassion on you. Rather you were thrown out into the open field, for you were abhorred on the day you were born. When I passed by you and saw you squirming in your blood, I said to you while you were in your blood, 'Live!' Yes, I said to you while you were in your blood, 'Live!'"*

While we were in our birth blood [earthly] dying and ignored, Christ brought the dying to life with His blood. He was speaking of the Israelites, but it applies to any who call upon the name of the Lord. We are all dying in our perishable blood. Without His blood replacement, we are doomed.

In Ephesians 2 above, Paul is talking about the natural uniting of Jews and Gentiles. Notwithstanding, the Word tells us the flesh is at enmity with the Spirit, and the Spirit is at enmity with the flesh. When we merge as one with God, hostility is put to death because our flesh is put to death. We are united.

"For this reason a man shall leave his father and mother and shall be joined to his wife, and the two shall become one flesh," reads Ephesians 5:31. This speaks about marriage in a human sense. Again, flipping it to our relationship with God [since everything on Earth is fashioned after God and our spiritual relationship with Him], He left His Father to join His wife, the Bride of Christ [us]. He forsook all to unite His bride unto Himself. He gave to His wife His essence, His Holy Spirit.

When we *"eat of His flesh and drink of His blood,"* we become one flesh with Christ, or better stated, we become one being, supernatural as He is supernatural. This marriage with Christ is where all His power and authority come into our possession. What is ours becomes His, and what is His becomes ours. I Corinthians breaks it down even more. He likens our relationship with Christ as marriage and becoming one flesh. To be a member of a body as we are with Christ means there has been a merger, a becoming one. Our legs are attached to our arms through the mid-section, and so on. They are all part of one body.

This is why we should not be conscienceless committing acts of sin once born-again. When we do, God calls it prostitution. In the natural, if a spouse cheats with another person, it is called adultery, harlotry, and prostitution. We are married to Christ and have become one flesh. Because of the Israelite's adultery and prostitution, of which the Old Testament speaks, they brought sudden death upon many by the wrath of God.

Take the controversy of Christians smoking; something familiar to everyone whether they or someone they know partakes. Is there a Scripture that reads, "Thou shall not smoke"? No, but many read we are the temple of the Most High God, and we are not to harm the body in any way. It is a holy temple in which His Spirit resides. Any of the following Scriptures will do nicely. When we understand how to have a reverent, holy fear of our Creator, we will not take the abuse of His temple lightly.

One Body:

"Do you know that your bodies are members of Christ? Shall I then take away the members of Christ and make them members of a prostitute? May it never be. Or do you not know that the one who joins himself to a prostitute is one body with her? For He says, 'The two shall become one flesh' (I Corinthians 6:15)."

"...through which the world has been crucified to me, and I to the world (Galatians 6:14)."

Therefore we have been buried with Him through baptism into death (depiction of drowning the ways of the world with your flesh), so that as Christ was raised from the dead through the glory of the Father, so we too might walk in newness of life with Him in the likeness of His death, certainly we shall also be in the likeness of His resurrection, knowing this, that our old self was crucified with Him, in order that our body of sin might be done away with, so that we would no longer be slaves to sin; *for he who has died is freed from sin.* Now if we have died with Christ, we believe that we shall also live with Him, knowing that Christ, having been raised from the dead, is never to die again; death no longer is master over Him. For the death that He died, He died to sin once for all; but the life that He lives, He lives to God. Even so, consider yourselves to be dead to sin, but alive to God in Christ Jesus (Romans 6:4-11).

That last sentence in Romans, "...*consider yourselves to be dead to sin, but alive to God in Christ Jesus,*" stumps most believers. We stand pure, holy, blameless, and sinless before the Father because the redemptive blood is that upon which God looks. This does not mean we never carry out an act of sin, but it is covered, past, present, and future.

Choice

Also, we have a conscious awareness of God at all times because of Holy Spirit in us, so we can pull down sin before it manifests.

His Spirit dwells in us. When I live in my physical home, all of me lives there. I don't send my toe or hand or any other part separate from the rest to reside. It is the same with Jesus Christ. He "*dwells, lives, resides, has made His abode*" in us—all of Him in all of us. That means He does not live in us in part, but in whole. To reiterate, why would anyone who reveres God purposely do anything to offend Him? We are aliens and strangers living in a land foreign to us because it is foreign to Christ. We are to live as Christ.

> "If Christ is in you, though the body is dead because of sin... the Spirit...dwells in you...(Romans 8:10-12)."

> "I have been crucified with Christ therefore I no longer live, but Christ lives in me...(Galatians 2:20)."

What can wash away my sin) nothing but the blood of Jesus -

Chapter 14

The Testimony

We all need desperately to know that the testimony of Christ is within the believer. It is how we boldly speak the truth, as did Paul, Peter, John the Baptist, and many others. Why did the disciples who walked every day with Jesus, the same who witnessed miracles and performed them, still suffer from unbelief? The Word reveals that even moments after they witnessed Jesus and His miracles firsthand, they still had doubt and unbelief.

The answer is simple. They had not yet received the anointing of Holy Spirit that occurred in the upper room (Acts 2). Jesus was still external. The disciples were led by their souls instead of their spirits. Holy Spirit is He who quickens a person's spirit to life. Without the quickening, there is no life, hence, no intimate communion with Him. Spirit communes with spirit. It is the same with Adam in the Garden. He walked and talked with God daily, yet sinned against Him because Holy Spirit was external instead of internal.

As I covered in-depth in my book, *What Was God Thinking: Why Adam Had to Die*, the only way to understand how God operates is for God Himself to be in us and overtake us. Our human nature, which is wicked and corrupt from birth, must die. With death, the life of Jesus Christ can be brought in. Only God can comprehend God. Neither Adam nor the disciples could understand God until God was within.

Once the disciples received Holy Spirit, they did go out and do greater things than Jesus. With Holy Spirit inserted into ourselves, His testimony is alive in us. This is how any disciple, past, present, or future, can have the supernatural ability to truly testify of Christ without wavering. Basically, Jesus Christ testifies for Himself through our obedience to the death of earthly nature.

If Christ's testimony, who is Jesus Christ —The Testimony—is in us, there can, in fact, be modern-day apostles and prophets. First, Paul would not have mentioned the five-fold ministry starting with the apostle and prophet if it were invalid to any generation between then and the second coming. Secondly, if the apostleship qualification is to have walked with Jesus and witnessed Him personally, who better than someone who has Christ inserted within? Jesus can testify for Himself through the willing vessel. It's far superior to walk *in* Jesus than merely *beside* Him.

Revelation 12:10-12 says, "*Now have come the salvation and the power and the kingdom of our God, and the authority of His Christ. For the accuser of our brethren has been thrown down, he who accuses them before our God day and night. And they overcame him by of the blood of the Lamb and because of the word of their testimony, and they did not love their life even when faced with death. For this reason, rejoice, O heavens and you who dwell in them. Woe to the Earth and the sea, because the devil has come down to you, having great wrath, knowing that he has only a short time.*" Also, in I John 5:10, we see, "*The one who believes in the Son of God has the testimony in himself...*"

Day of the Lord:

> And I will grant wonders in the sky above and signs on the Earth below, blood, and fire, and vapor of smoke. The sun will be turned into darkness and the moon into blood, before the great and glorious day of the Lord shall come. And it shall be that everyone who calls on the name of the Lord will be saved (Acts 2:19-21).

> "…they have washed their robes and made them white in the blood of the Lamb (Revelation 7:14)."

As God has revealed, the blood that will come and cover the moon is the very lifeblood of Christ displayed for all to see. His holy blood is not red. It is white, as stated in Revelation. It was undoubtedly depicted as red or scarlet on the Earth because He took on man's blood. In fact, man's blood is red for a very significant reason; red is the most difficult color to get out of anything. When I decorated cakes, the red dye was incredibly difficult to clean as red stains are worse than any other. Ladies, have you ever tried to remove red lipstick from your lips? It won't even wipe off. It has to wear off. Have you ever spilled red juice or wine on cloth? Generally, it will not come out without bleaching.

The color red represents the stains of our sins that will not come out without the pure, white blood of Christ to replace it. His blood does not just cover but removes and replaces. In the heavenly realm, Jesus' blood is pure and whiter than snow. This is why the sun, the natural light of Earth, will be darkened. The moon, which comes out in the darkness, will be lit with the holy, unblemished, white blood of Christ. Light shines brightest in the darkness. Only the moon can be seen in the day and night as the sun is never seen in the dark of night.

Prayer:

With a sincere heart before You, Jesus, I pray that You will truly wash me with the water that ran from Your side, allow Your Spirit to move into my now purified body, and seal me with Your holy, pure blood. I thank You, Father, that now I am, without question, a child of the King. Show me continually how to be perfected in You, how to rest in You who is Rest, and allow You to move through me instead of me "*doing*" work in the flesh. Show me how to die daily to my flesh so that You never be quenched within me. Allow me, O God, to be as a poured-out drink offering, a fragrance that is a sweet aroma to Your nostrils as my fat is burned in sacrifice to You, my righteous Husband. Allow me to be a part of Your bride without spot or wrinkle. I love You, Jesus. May I ever grow more deeply in love with You over time. I dedicate my life to You, yielded and consecrated before You."

Notes

Chapter 15

Can Salvation Be Lost?

For in the case of those who have once been enlightened and have tasted of the heavenly gift and have been made partakers of the Holy Spirit, and have tasted the good word of God and the powers of the age to come, and then have fallen away, it is impossible to renew them again to repentance, since they again crucify to themselves the Son of God and put Him to open shame. For ground that drinks the rain which often falls on it and brings forth vegetation useful to those for whose sake it is also tilled, receives a blessing from God; but if it yields thorns and thistles, it is worthless and close to being cursed, and it ends up being burned (Hebrews 6:4-6).

"Therefore I say to you, any sin and blasphemy shall be forgiven people but blasphemy against the Spirit shall not be forgiven. Whoever speaks a word against the Son of Man, it shall be forgiven him; but whoever speaks against the Holy Spirit, it shall not be forgiven him, either in this age or in the age to come (Matthew 12:31-32)."

And just as they did not see fit to acknowledge God any longer, God gave them over to a depraved mind, to do those things which are not proper, being filled with all unrighteousness...although they know the ordinance of God, that those who practice such things are worthy of death, they not only do the same, but also give hearty approval to those who practice them (Romans 1:28-32).

"Keeping faith and a good conscience, which some have rejected and suffered shipwreck in regard to their faith. Among these are Hymenaeus and Alexander, whom I have handed over to Satan, so that they will be taught not to blaspheme (I Timothy 1:19-20)."

It is a trustworthy statement...if we deny Him, He also will deny us; if we are faithless, He remains faithful, for He cannot deny Himself (II Timothy 2:11-13).

"Not a novice, lest being lifted up with pride he fall into the condemnation of the devil (I Timothy 3:6, KJV)."

Two Groups:

This is a topic highly discussed and argued from generation to generation. Many have spoken boldly that, once saved, always saved, no matter what. This particular group says that it diminishes the power of the blood to say eternal salvation can be lost. Then there are the people who believe you can get it, lose it, get it again, lose it again, and so on. They seem to believe salvation is something that can come and go with the wind. I must admit that I don't fully understand that thinking as I am not sure which sins would constitute losing salvation and which ones would not.

As I have heard both perspectives throughout my many years as a follower of Christ, I decided to check it out for myself, and here is what I found. Please read the text above very closely to investigate and ponder for yourself. I didn't want to exclude any, though they are lengthy. I wanted to give a solid foundation for what I am going to state next. Look especially at the first reference, Hebrews chapter 6.

From all this, here is my conclusion. No one can *"lose"* their salvation as one would a set of car keys. It can, however, be *"removed"* by the one who possesses it. These Scriptures seem to discredit both theories stated in the first paragraph. One, salvation can be forfeited, and two, if forfeited, it is not something one can regain. This seems very clear to me. We do not serve a wishy-washy God. He is stable, steadfast, and sure in all His ways. I would not want a God who dangles eternal salvation in my face just to take it away every time I make a misstep. Thankfully, He is not that kind of God. He is loving, patient, kind, and faithful.

"No Snatch" Clause:

My sheep hear My voice, and I know them, and they follow Me; and I give eternal life to them, and they will never perish; and no one will snatch them out of My hand. My Father who has given them to Me, is greater than all; and no one is able to snatch them out of the Father's hand (John 10:27-29).

Many people's argument is the text in John chapter 10 where no man can snatch a person out of God's hand. I have heard and even quoted, *"No one can snatch me from the hand of God, including me."* However, here is what I found. If a person blasphemes Holy Spirit, they are choosing to forfeit their covenant with God the Father. They are saying what Satan himself roughly said in heaven, *"I am better than You, God, and I reject You fully."* I cannot conceive of this, yet the Word is proof positive it can, in fact, happen.

I give my perspective, not to be argumentative, but rather to aid God's people in balance. I have spoken with countless Christians who live in constant fear they have done something so wrong that, maybe, they lost their eternal salvation. God's people are living in fear. Fear stunts growth past the point of salvation because they are too busy getting *"saved"* over and over. Fear, in this instance, is satanic instead of holy, reverent fear of God. This topic is, as Paul states, elementary.

Satan keeps God's people defeated within their own minds. He may not be able to take away our salvation, but he can keep us so bound in fear of losing salvation that we never mature in Christ. If we never grow, we are incapable of assisting the growth of others. If we aren't confident in where and who we are in Christ, how can we be a strong witness to anyone else? This is why it is elementary. It is the ABCs of God. We all need to grow into learning how to form sentences with the elemental things and then on to entire conversations, figuratively speaking.

I have no problem with those who think they cannot lose salvation through any means. As long as they continue in their walk seeking Holy Spirit leading, the topic is moot. Also, for those who think salvation can come and go, this will hopefully help balance them eliminating the nature of fear so to mature in Christ. Fear comes from always thinking we will mess up too much and be doomed to hell. Salvation, in this way, would be based on works instead of grace. It is vital to know the truth of the Word to stay in proper balance in Christ.

In Hebrews and Matthew, we read that to blaspheme the Son is forgivable, but the only unforgivable sin is to blaspheme Holy Spirit. The best way I can describe this is to completely turn our backs on God, as did Lucifer. Lucifer had such a bitter heart of pride that he wanted to be God. In other words, to overthrow God and steal His glory saying, "*I know You are real, but I want nothing to do with You.*"

It isn't so much unbelief of God, but something worse. It is to believe and reject anyway. This is how Satan blasphemed the very Spirit of God by saying, "*I want nothing to do with You or Your ways. I want to replace You.*" Let's face it, Lucifer tasted God and all His goodness more than any mortal. He ruled in the Earth on the high mountain of God and in the Garden of Eden. Nevertheless, with all that, he turned his back to God with utter hatred. Basically, he forfeited a "*God-consciousness.*"

We all know and accept there is nothing that can be prayed on Satan's behalf that would allow him reentry to God, and so it is with those who have "*tasted the good word of God and the powers of the age to come, and then have fallen away.*" A person who could know with intense intimacy the goodness of God and turn away would have to be someone with irreversible pride and hardness of heart. This is not necessarily someone, for instance, who sins even unto murder.

It is a sin against Jesus Christ to commit murder, lies, thievery, cheating, suicide, adultery, homosexuality, gossip, whatever. These, on their own, are not unforgivable because it is not sinning against Holy Spirit. On the other hand, if we know these things are sinful—having once been intimate with God, yet we do them with total disregard of conviction, it constitutes sin against His Spirit. For that, there is no further forgiveness. The Scripture in I Timothy chapter one further confirms this. It speaks of those who had walked with God but then shipwrecked and abandoned their faith. These people were turned over to Satan due to their blatant blasphemy.

In short, to blaspheme Holy Spirit is to have no consciousness of God whatsoever. Here is the reference of the clause *"no one can pluck them from My hand."* This type person who blasphemes Holy Spirit isn't *"plucked,"* but instead, they walk away. No one *"snatched"* them as would a thief stealing an item. They simply walked away of their own volition, a total forfeiture from a reprobate mind.

LOST?

Who turns their backs on God?

Who knows ones HEART — ?

blasphemy

blatant blasphemy

PRIDE — hardness of the heart

*Sin against Holy Spirit

Chapter 16

Have I Blasphemed Holy Spirit?

For in the case of those who have once been enlightened and have tasted of the heavenly gift and have been made partakers of the Holy Spirit, and have tasted the good word of God and the powers of the age to come, and then have fallen away, it is impossible to renew them again to repentance, since they again crucify to themselves the Son of God and put Him to open shame. For ground that drinks the rain which often falls on it and brings forth vegetation useful to those for whose sake it is also tilled, receives a blessing from God; but if it yields thorns and thistles, it is worthless and close to being cursed, and it ends up being burned (Hebrews 6:4-6).

If you ever wondered if you have blasphemed Holy Spirit, you have not. If you had, you would not care or to pose the question. To care one way or the other proves you still have a God-consciousness to some degree. All you need to do is confess and repent of whatever caused you to ask the question, and forgiveness belongs to you. Go and sin no more.

I love the analogy in Hebrews where the rain falls on the ground as a blessing. Growth comes from rain. If the growth is thorns and thistles, it is basically cursed and will be burned in the fire. The *"growth"* was corrupt, although the "rain" God sent was pure. As Holy Spirit rains into our spirit-man, abundance is bound to come. If Holy Spirit is the One in control, good fruit will manifest. If the recipient's heart turns brittle toward the rain and its giver, evil [thorns and thistles] will arise in the place of righteousness [good fruit]. The fire that will burn that person and their wicked deeds is the holy fire of God. Remember, when holy fire comes from heaven, wood, hay, and stubble will be burned, but the gold and precious stones will be refined.

Many people want to argue this with me. I speak on this topic simply to clarify what constitutes *"losing salvation."* Technically, it cannot be lost, but, as I have stated, it can be forfeited [willingly relinquished]. It is a complete and utter turning away from Christ. I have had many Scriptures tossed at me, such as Romans 8:1, which states there is now no condemnation in Christ Jesus, but it only further confirmed my stance. The latter part of the text reads, *"…for those who are led by the Spirit and not the flesh."* Here we are again with Holy Spirit. For those who allow Holy Spirit leading, there is no condemnation. Reject Holy Spirit leading, and condemnation ensue.

Then there is Romans 1:14-17, which roughly reads that those who are led by Holy Spirit are the sons of God. Romans 8:14 states, *"For all who are being led by the Spirit of God, these are sons of God."* To say it simply, no Holy Spirit equals *"not a son."* So, whether we never received salvation necessary to receive the gift of Holy Spirit or we have but then turned away by blaspheming Holy Spirit, we are not a son. Notice in the verses below where we are told to *"remain in Him"* as though it is our choice whether or not we remain. Those who choose not to stay in Him are like the branch tossed and burned in the fire.

> I am the true vine, and My Father is the vinedresser. Every branch in Me that does not bear fruit, He takes away; and every branch that bears fruit, He prunes it so that it may bear more fruit. You are already clean because of the word which I have spoken to you. Abide in Me, and I in you. As the branch cannot bear fruit of itself unless it abides in the vine, so neither can you unless you abide in Me. I am the vine, you are the branches; he who abides in Me and I in him, he bears much fruit, for apart from Me you can do nothing. If anyone does not abide in Me, he is thrown away as a branch and dries up; and they gather them, and cast them into the fire and they are burned. If you abide in Me, and My words abide in you, ask whatever you wish and it will be done for you. My Father is glorified by this, that you bear much fruit, and so prove to be My disciples. Just as the Father has loved Me, I have also loved you; abide in My love…these things I have spoken to you so that My joy may be in you, and that your joy may be made full (John 15:1-9, 11).

My biggest issue in all this is not whether eternal salvati forfeited but that Christians want to argue the forget Jesus calls us never to be argumentative with one another. I have had brothers and sis speaking to me because of this very topic. It is no wonder the Bride of Christ has not been taken—we have not become spotless or wrinkle-free. There is perpetual hatred among believers.

Christians, as a whole, would dispute this point of view spending endless hours trying to prove others wrong rather than just going on about the Father's business making disciples of many nations. For those who believe we can never lose it and for those who think we can gain and lose it repeatedly, I love them and commune with them when they are willing. I have no desire to change their minds. I just want to bring some peace and clarity to those who want to know.

May we all be more focused on unity within the Body of Christ and Kingdom expansion than trying to argue against one another. Besides, so long as we are unwilling to blaspheme Holy Spirit purposing to walk according to the Spirit, the issue is of no consequence. It is evident in Luke 11:5-13 that if we ask for Holy Spirit, God will surely freely give Him. Once we have asked and received, if we then turn and reject Him, how could God give Him again? To blaspheme Holy Spirit leaves one unconcerned with losing Him or ever receiving Him again.

Notes

Chapter 17

Who Is Holy Spirit?

"Peter said to them, 'Repent, and each of you be baptized in the name of Jesus Christ for the forgiveness of your sins; and you will receive the gift of the Holy Spirit' (Acts 2:38)."

...the one who confesses the Son has the Father also...this is the promise which He Himself made to us; eternal life...as for you, the anointing which you received from Him abides in you, and you have no need for anyone to teach you; but as His anointing teaches you about all things, and is true and is not a lie...(I John 2:23, 25, 27).

"But you will receive power when the Holy Spirit has come upon you; and you shall be my witnesses...even to the remotest part of the Earth (Acts 1:8)."

"When they arrest you and hand you over, do not worry beforehand about what you are to say, but say whatever is given you in that hour; for it is not you who speak, but it is the Holy Spirit (Mark 13:11)."

"... He will give you another Helper, that He may be with you forever; that is the Spirit of truth, whom the world cannot receive, because it does not see Him or know Him, but you know Him because He abides with you and will be in you (John 14:15-16)."

"You know of Jesus of Nazareth, how God anointed Him with the Holy Spirit and with power, and how He went about doing good and healing all who were oppressed by the devil, for God was with Him (Acts 10:38)."

Definition of Anointing: to smear or rub with oil

*I*n short, Holy Spirit is the heart of God. He is the "*fat*" that covers, constantly lubricating our hearts, souls, and spirits. He is the anointing of which we read so much in the Word. He is the Comforter, the down payment of things to come. II Corinthians 1:22 reads, "*...set His seal of ownership on us, and put His Spirit in our hearts as a deposit, guaranteeing what is to come.*" Holy Spirit is God's pledge to those who receive Him, that whatever He promises for this life and the next, He will not renege.

Holy Spirit is as a wedding ring from a man to his bride. He, God, is our Groom, and believers are His bride. Holy Spirit is a down payment [a guarantee] for what is to be hers through holy matrimony. A ring signifies love and covenant between the giver and the recipient.

It is a *"symbol of ownership,"* and no one else has the right to take her. Holy Spirit within the believer is the symbol to Satan that the person belongs to God and he is not to touch them in any way outside God's permission.

If a married woman is out and a man sees her ring attempting to pick her up, she can count on her husband stepping in assuring that the other guy knows to whom she belongs. Holy Spirit acts on God's behalf as our "marital *signet ring*," a sign of belonging. Without Him outwardly—active from within the body, how will the enemy and his legion of demons—active from without the body—know to whom we belong? We must allow our inward Ring to be seen through our external conduct.

Every born-again believer has been given Holy Spirit. The problem enters when we don't know anything about Him, His function in our daily lives, or how to operate in His power and authority. Without Holy Spirit in operation in the life of the person of God, it is like a wife going out without her wedding ring. It leaves her vulnerable to the enemy because of the lack of an outward mark of belonging even though covenant is still present. Furthermore, if we are not confident and grounded in the significance of the covenant the ring represents, we can still fall prey to the enemy's attack.

I became born-again at the age of six. The only time I ever heard the name *"Holy Spirit"* was at physical baptism. That doesn't mean it wasn't mentioned, but that's where I remember it significantly. It wasn't until the age of 30 that I began to hear of His indwelling and how He is to operate through me. That is a shame and disgrace to God. Everyone around me was busy talking about *"getting saved* [from hell]" but never did they talk about the insertion of Holy Spirit and what that meant. No one seemed to understand the Kingdom of God. It stands to reason they didn't and couldn't understand the offshoot of God's Kingdom [salvation, Holy Spirit, covenant, love, and so on].

In the references above, we see that, with Holy Spirit, we don't need a teacher because Holy Spirit will teach and guide us. Yes, we need teachers in the natural, but this means once a person is really attuned to Holy Spirit on a mature level, He will give all instruction, whether through His anointed authority or directly. We cannot understand the Word through anointed people lest we are in tune with the same Spirit. Only Holy Spirit can open someone allowing them to understand the information being fed. With that, we won't feel the need to be confirmed or solidified by a human when we make decisions based on His leading. When we stand accused before our enemies, we don't have to panic. Holy Spirit will speak through our mouths. He is our confidence in all things at all times. It is quite an extraordinary life led by Holy Spirit. I never knew how remarkable life could be in Christ.

When I first began to understand Holy Spirit, I was mad that no one at church taught me. Then, as I began to grow, I had to recognize that the Word of God was always at my disposal. It was *my* obligation to check the Word myself. Once I was of an age I could read, I was of an age to comprehend His written Word if I allowed Holy Spirit to interpret. I simply chose not to investigate on my own. I have no one to blame but myself. Yes, those who knew and did not tell me are accountable before God, but I, the individual person, am always accountable for my own actions or lack thereof.

Because of this, it is my most earnest desire to get the Word out about Father, Son, and Holy Spirit and all He reveals so I will not be accountable for the blood of those whom I could have touched. Whether people receive or not, listen or don't, I will stand erect before Almighty God one day knowing I did what I was called to do on Earth. God's people are perishing for lack of knowledge. The more God's people understand His Word, the more people can be saved from not only hell, but this perverse generation.

Where to Begin?

Pray for Holy Spirit to teach us. We are to get in line with Holy Spirit allowing His presence to overtake us with His wisdom, knowledge, understanding, and all that is within Him. Begin to proclaim His promises are *"yes"* and *"amen."* Make declarations that the only voice we will hear is that of God commanding the voice of Satan to be silenced. We possess the authority to speak against demonic activity with the same power that raised Christ from the dead when in obedience to Holy Spirit.

"The Helper" is Holy Spirit, so allow Him to help. We should ask God to quicken our spirits to life so that we can clearly see, hear, know and understand His Word. I repeat that Holy Spirit communes with our spirit, not our soul. He saves our soul by igniting our spirit. He teaches our spirit to control the soul, hence directing the outer shell of flesh. We belong to Christ because we have been bought with a price. We bear His signet ring [Holy Spirit]. He is to dictate our purpose on this Earth and what our focus should be. We have no say in the matter except, *"Let the mind that is in Christ be also in me."*

Remember, you and I are to be born of water and Spirit and blood. This is not physical water baptism. This is the holy water that ran from the side of Jesus with the blood about which we spoke earlier. As a recap, when we choose death to the flesh, Holy Spirit sends His water to cleanse our inner man. Then He places His Spirit in the clean place inside our empty shell. Afterward, He takes His pure blood sealing Holy Spirit in the clean place as Holy Spirit cannot live in a dirty temple. Though we may sin, Holy Spirit is not defiled. Instead, He instructs our spirit the sin, and we must confess and repent. A person genuinely washed by the water, filled with Holy Spirit, and sealed with His blood will purpose to not sin. Sin will merely be an act of ignorance, not consciousness.

In this, we will understand better about physical baptism. It is exclusively the baptism of the Holy Spirit that extends eternal life to know the Father and the Son (John 17). The only way to know the Trinity is to have Him inserted within. That is the epitome of intimacy [oneness]. All the arguments of total emersion versus sprinkling will become irrelevant. The baptism of which God speaks is not of the flesh [outer man] but of the spirit [inner man]. Physical baptism is merely an outward display of what has happened internally, so what difference does it make to be dunked or sprinkled? One drop of His holy water and blood can cover the entire universe. We all need to get past how things appear physically [surface] and pray to have supernatural vision into God's sight [the deep root].

Prayer:

In the holy name of Jesus Christ, I pray for the natural to become unnatural and the supernatural of God to become natural. Give me eyes to see, ears to hear, and a mind to understand and comprehend

Your Word. Show me how to be led only of, by, and through the power of the Holy Spirit within. Burn everything within me that was not planted there by You, O Lord. Show me how to walk, talk and think like You. Let the mind that is in Christ be also in me. Reveal to me my kingdom purpose on this planet that I may, through Your power within, fulfill it. You are my heart and my desire. On Your word, I meditate day and night. May You always correct me when I make a misstep. Teach me, O God, to move past the elementary things of Your Word so that I will move into the real richness of all You have ordained for, by, and through me. Help me not focus on the fear of losing salvation or forfeiting it, but rather, help me focus entirely on falling in love with You and pleasing You. I love You, Lord. Allow me the privilege of falling in love with You as You are in love with me. Show me how to reciprocate Your love.

Notes

Chapter 18

The Enemy Called "Depression"

For though we live in this world, we do not wage war as the world does. The weapons we fight with are not the weapons of the world. On the contrary, they have divine power to demolish strongholds. We demolish arguments and every pretension that sets itself up against the knowledge of God, and we take captive every thought to make it obedient to Christ. And we will be ready to punish every act of disobedience, once your obedience is complete (II Corinthians 10:3-6).

Dethroning Satan:

When we grasp the reality of Satan understanding he is truly out to destroy those whom God loves, we will better understand we need to stand as closely *in* Jesus as possible. Satan is a powerful source against those who do not perceive he is dead and that God is at the helm of everything. Once we recognize God is all-in-all intending everything to work together for our good if we love

Him, the tool of deception will no longer have the ability to overtake us.

The devil is only as powerful as we allow. Satan has no dominion over God's bride without her permission. Scripture after Scripture repeats that we are released from Satan's stronghold by God's power [Holy Spirit within]. We simply need to know the tools of authority God has provided and how to utilize them. With such power from God, why do we allow Satan to oppress us? No matter where we are in life or our walk with Christ, depression seems to be a main element attacking followers of Christ at some point. It would behoove us all to learn the nature of depression, and that its author is the father of lies. SATAN

Depression and heaviness come from a disobedient thought pattern stemming from being disillusioned by the enemy's lie. This is called a *"stronghold."* Depression in the life of a son of God is like taking off our signet ring. I can't quote II Corinthians 10:3-6 enough. Our every thought needs to be in perfect alignment with God. Depression comes from selfish thoughts and self-pity. As born-again believers, we are to put away selfish thoughts and desires. We are to be a bondservant, serving one another, thinking of others above ourselves. When we are in a perpetual state of self-pity [depression], we give away our ability to serve because we only focus on ourselves and how others should serve us. We're locked into all things we are missing; the things we want but don't have, have but don't' want, and all the issues of life making us downtrodden. Depression stems from feeling sorry for ourselves and our unpleasant circumstances. It is the opposite of focusing on *"whatsoever is pure, holy and of good report."*

Philippians 4:8

Fruit of the Spirit:

> "But the fruit of the Spirit is love, joy, peace, patience, kindness, goodness, faithfulness, gentleness and self-control (Galatians 5:22-23)."

God's people should be self-controlled and self-disciplined, not led by emotions—our own or those around us. Being manipulated by emotions is the opposite of being controlled by the Holy Spirit. Depression is of the enemy, Satan, not of the Spirit of the One True God. Depression is the enemy of holiness, fruitfulness, purity, and the joy of the Lord. Galatians 5 lists many characteristics of one fruit. It is the *"fruit"* [singular] of the Spirit, not *"fruits"* [plural].

Although I wrote in two previous books, *Looking for God* and *What Was God Thinking?*, it bears repeating as many times as possible: Holy Spirit [the Tree of Life] can only bear one type of fruit. E.g., apples can be plentiful on one tree, but they're still one apple type. All have the same description and identifiable markings. All characteristics come, not just one or a select few. Granted, just as one Red Delicious apple may be slightly redder or sweeter than another, all Red Delicious apples are basically the same with only minor variations. So it is with people led by Holy Spirit. We may be stronger or weaker in certain areas compared to another person led by Holy Spirit, but all Spirit led people are basically the same in nature.

If we genuinely bear the fruit of the Spirit, we will operate in all attributes of that fruit. To produce anything other than this fruit type, what we bear is like the thorns and thistles mentioned previously. When we allow depression and self-pity to rule, we lose all the attributes of Holy Spirit. Read this next section to see the correlation between the characteristics of the genuine fruit and how, when one is absent, they all begin to vanish:

1. Give up self-control to emotionalism.

2. Goodness leaves because emotionalism oppresses Holy Spirit—goodness comes only from the Spirit of God ruling.

3. We lose kindness when we wallow in self-pity. We aren't even kind to ourselves; therefore, lose the ability to show kindness to others.

4. We lose patience, which most people generally lack because they don't look to Holy Spirit to produce patience. Frustration accompanies self-pity and impatience, so we become agitated and short with everyone and everything.

5. Obviously, there is no peace with self-pity and depression. If we had the peace that God freely gives, we would be free of depression. Peace is the opposite of depression.

6. Joy transcends everything negative. Joy is what God gives despite our circumstances. Joy is inner peace even when we are not happy about what is happening. Happiness is based on the things happening around us and is led by the soul [mind, will, emotions]. Joy is driven by the Spirit regardless of circumstances.

7. Gentleness is absent because depression aggravates us. When we are agitated, we are unkind to others and, in turn, lack gentleness, kindness, and love. We become abrupt with others due to our dissatisfaction with life.

Psalm 41:3

8. We are of a disobedient mindset while in a state of depression. When we are wayward in any area, we cannot be faithful to the will of God. Disobedience is total self-absorption.

9. When depressed, we are in an absolute state of hatred, hating ourselves, our circumstances, situations, sometimes even God. This admits to God that we believe He has somehow forsaken us. This means we are calling God a liar. Love begins with God, and it should first be applied to self. If we have no love for ourselves, how would it be beneficial to "*love others as yourself*"?

10. Self-absorption causes depression and squelches anything of God. We cannot focus on the goodness of God because we're too honed into how neglected we feel. Depression overrides everything of Holy Spirit. It bears only thorns and thistles, whereas Holy Spirit bears only good fruit.

With All Your Heart, Soul, Mind and Strength:

"Love the Lord our God, the Lord is one. Love the Lord your God with all your heart and all your soul and all of your mind and with all your strength. The second is this: Love your neighbor as yourself. There is no commandment greater than these (Mark 12:30-31)."

God must expect us to love ourselves if He compares it to loving our neighbor. Without Holy Spirit at the helm, we cannot bear good fruit. If we do not bear good fruit, we cannot conduct ourselves in the characteristics of God. After all, that's what the fruit of the

Spirit is—the very nature of God. Without bearing His fruit, we bear thorns and weeds, leading us to wither away. Instead of good fruit, the rain of the Holy Spirit waters the bitterness and anger we are holding in our hearts. The result is thorns and thistles leaving us as good as cursed (Hebrews 6:4-6).

Depression causes one to become ineffective for Christ and the Kingdom of God. Depression is one of the most selfish acts of sin a person can commit. It stems from the root of pride as all thoughts and actions are centered on self. That sin leads to others such as adultery, fornication, homosexuality, suicide, lying, stealing, coveting, murder, confusion, gossip, slander, murmuring, complaining, and much of the like. The act of sin always comes from first meditating exclusively on what we desire versus what God desires. Pride is the root of depression and all sin.

These acts of heart-sin are the equivalent of weeds that choke Holy Spirit anointing. Just as natural weeds overtake a garden of ripe fruit and vegetables, so it is with the believer. If we don't daily check the gardens of our hearts pruning pride, the harmful growth will overshadow and destroy the good seed.

One sin leads to another. When we are operating in pride only thinking of ourselves, we cannot think about the things of God. We cannot think of what is right, but only what will bring a quick fix to our flesh. Our thinking becomes foggy and jumbled, harsh and damaging. Confusion enters, and then we wonder if God really exists or if He really loves us. God is not the author of confusion. Satan is. We need to pull down imaginations and strongholds from our minds by the authority Jesus gave us when He rose from the grave. This is "making your body a slave" to the righteousness of Christ. When we love the Lord our God with the entirety of our hearts, souls, minds, and strength, there is nothing left to feed selfishness. In this condition, depression cannot live.

Case in Point:

When my daughter was chronically ill many years, we did everything spiritually and physically we knew to do, so we waited upon the Lord. It would have been easy for us to become depressed attempting to understand why God immediately enacts healing on some but not her. Nevertheless, we chose to stay our minds on the litany of God's miracles and blessings He had bestowed us over the years. We chose to focus on all the personal *"whatsoever is of good report"* in our lives.

I can't help but recall that Sophia was, as were her previous seven siblings, dead in my womb. Knowing my pregnancy with her was like all the others, God sent prayer warriors to speak His life into her while in my womb. God chose to raise her from the dead allowing her to live. Knowing this as a fact, how could I have possibly allowed depression to enter our lives? By keeping our thoughts on Jesus and His goodness, there was no room for depression to take root.

Sure, I will be the first to admit that there were pockets of weakness where I couldn't help but wonder, *"Why, Lord, do You not raise Sophia from her sickbed? We have declared, decreed, repented, anointed with oil, had elders lay hands upon her, bound demons, released Holy Spirit, proclaimed her healing, and more. We have changed our diet and taken the appropriate medications according to the instructions of medical professionals. Why Lord?"*

In that train of thought, Holy Spirit quickened my mind back to the reality of heaven, back to the goodness of God. He reminded me that He forewarned me of the trials to come in which we found ourselves. He encouraged me in my spirit to stay the course and that every person's journey is different, yet always with the directive of strengthening us for the real battles that lie ahead. God is faithful in all He does, all He allows, and in all, He purposes for the eventual good of His people. Depression has no room in the life of those regenerated in the blood of Jesus. Refuse unapologetically to be conformed to the mindset of this temporal, condemned world.

Notes

Chapter 19

CNonconformist

"Do not conform any longer to the pattern of this world, but be transformed by the renewing of your mind. Then you will be able to test and approve what God's will is – His good, pleasing and perfect will (**Romans 12:2**)."

"*Do not conform any longer...*" This indicates that we are naturally conformed to the world, but we retain the option to cease. We need to renew our minds daily from being underneath the thinking of this condemned world. We ought not let Satan crowd us. Everything seems cloudy when depression is present. We need to have a full view of God's clear will. Take up the Jesus Christ-given authority commanding the spirit of depression to leave. We do not have to stay under its heaviness. Rise above it because we who are in Christ are seated at the right hand of God with Jesus in the heavenlies.

Claim what Christ has already said is ours. Get help. We are not to allow shame [pride] to keep us from receiving the proper help. We are one body and should help one another without shame or fear of what others may think. The Word of God directs us how to over-come depression because God understands the nature of the flesh is prideful and selfish by natural birth. We shouldn't feel ashamed when we sense depression coming but ought to recognize it as an enemy's attack. We must gird our loins and team with folks who understand how to help overcome the impulse of self-centeredness.

Spend time every day praising God. When we focus on praising Christ, we have no time for selfish thoughts. Praising God regardless of our circumstances confounds the enemy. Satan cannot compre-hend it. It is imperative to get our thinking aligned with God's. Seek to know his love's height, width, length, and depth because love cov-ers a multitude of sins. Begin speaking the answer to the problem instead of focusing on the problem. Stop saying, "*Woe is me*," and begin speaking, "*Praise God. I am healed spiritually, physically, mentally, emotionally, and financially.*" Claim the promises of God. Know what He offers and all that is available to us. Put on a garment of praise. I John 5:14-15 states, "*…ask anything in His name and we will receive the petitions according to His will.*"

God does not lie. When we seek a life free of satanic oppression of any kind, Yahweh is faithful to oblige. He more so wants us free than we wish ourselves free. He offered His Son as a sacrifice to give us freedom before we existed. We must position ourselves to receive what He graciously provided. Look at how King David han-dled depression:

> [David in the desert of Judah] Because Your love is better than life, my lips will glorify You. I will praise You as long as I live, and in Your name I will lift up my hands. My soul will

be satisfied as with the richest of foods; with singing lips my mouth will praise you. On my bed I remember You; I think of You through the watches of the night. Because You are my help, I sing in the shadow of Your wings. My soul clings to You; Your right hand upholds me (Psalm 63:3-8).

Notice David praised God for what he knew in his heart and mind. It is our experience and wisdom of the knowledge of God that saves us in troubled times. David was in the middle of a hot, dry, barren desert with no home or wife. Yet, with his lips and heart, he praised his God of salvation and redemption. David did not focus on the problem that would have allowed self-pity to enter his mind and heart. Instead, he focused on God, knowing full well He is faithful, gracious, and his help in time of need. At that, he did not stay in the desert. He came out becoming a mighty king.

Holy Spirit is our help, aid, comforter, guide, and the internal voice of God Almighty. Without Him, we crumble from brittle, dry bones. With Him, we are pliable, adaptable to any environment, and strengthened in every weakness to be equipped to conquer as one who is already victorious before the battle begins. Personally, I've learned to not only depend upon Holy Spirit but to enjoy His constant presence. When we choose to not conform to this world in all its pride [depression, self-loathing, self-absorption, and all things self-centered], Holy Spirit is free to move in and through us. This changes the world instead of the world-changing us.

Choose this day whom you will serve: the world and its corrupt order controlled by Satan or the Kingdom of God and its purity through Holy Spirit. Because of God's love, we possess the power of choice.

Finally, be strong in the Lord and in His mighty power. Put on the full armor of God so that you can take a stand against the devil's schemes. For our struggle is not against flesh and blood, but against the rulers, against the authorities, against the powers of this dark world and against the spiritual forces of evil in the heavenly realm. Therefore, put on the full armor of God, so that when the day of evil comes, you may be able to stand your ground, and after you have done everything, to stand. Stand firm then, with the belt of truth buckled around your waist, with the breastplate of righteousness in place and with your feet fitted with the readiness that comes from the gospel of peace. In addition to all this, take up the shield of faith, with which you can extinguish all the flaming arrows of the evil one. Take the helmet of salvation and the sword of the Spirit, which is the Word of God. And pray in the Spirit on all occasions with all kinds of prayers and requests. With this in mind, be alert and always keep on praying for all the saints (Ephesians 6:10-18).

"Surely He took up our infirmities and carried our sorrows (Isaiah 53:4)."

The Spirit of the Sovereign Lord is on Me, because the Lord has anointed Me to preach good news to the poor. He has sent Me to bind up the broken hearted, to proclaim freedom for the captives and release from darkness for the prisoners… to comfort all who mourn (Isaiah 61:1-3).

Notes

Introduction to Christ

*I*f you have come across this book, and you have never been properly introduced to God, this closing is a brief overview of how to come into the Kingdom of God.

Believe:

> "He then brought them out and asked, 'Sir, what must I do to be saved?' They replied, '*Believe in the Lord Jesus*, and you will be saved (Acts 16:29).'"

> "For John came to you to show you the way of righteousness, and you did not believe him, but the tax collectors and the prostitutes did. And even after you saw this, you did not repent and believe him (Matthew 21:32)."

"*For all have sinned and fall short of the glory of God*" is found in Romans 3:23. You must believe you dwell in a sinful nature derived from Adam and The Fall of mankind. Secondly, you must believe that Jesus is Lord, that He gave His life for sinful mankind [you] and accept His supernatural gift. It is simultaneously the easiest and hardest decision of anyone's life.

In response to such a belief in the Savior, you can take hold of this Scripture. *"Whosoever shall call on the name of the Lord shall be saved* (Acts 2:21)." You are *"whosoever."* Call out to Him – He's waiting.

Repentance Requirement:

"This is what is written: The Messiah will suffer and rise from the dead on the third day, and *repentance for the forgiveness of sins* will be preached in His name to all nations…(Luke 24:46-47)."

"Jesus answered them, 'It is not the healthy who need a doctor, but the sick. I have not come to call the righteous, but *sinners to repentance* (Luke 5:31-32)."

Repentance is a turning and returning. It is a turning away [turning your back] from one direction to another, and then turning toward God. It's an act of absolute humility—also a requirement for the presence of God to rest upon you. Repentance ushers God's grace through humility.

Baptism to Eternal Life:

"For *you have died* and your life is hidden with Christ in God (Colossians 3:3)."

"I baptize you with water, but He will *baptize you with the Holy Spirit* (Mark 1:8)."

"He who has believed and has been *baptized shall be saved*; but he who has disbelieved shall be condemned (Mark 16:16)."

"Therefore we have been *buried with Him through baptism into death*, so that as Christ was raised from the dead through the glory of the Father, so we too might walk in newness of life (Romans 6:4)."

"For all of you who were baptized into Christ have clothed yourselves with Christ (Galatians 3:27)."

Baptism takes belief a step further. Baptism, contrary to the modern-day church, *precedes* salvation not *succeeds*. This is not physical baptism, but spiritual. We are to surrender ourselves unto death in the spiritual sense to be able to receive a spiritual new life; hence the Scripture, "*I have been crucified in Christ; therefore it's no longer I who live but Christ who lives in me* (Galatians 2:20)."

Baptism, metaphorically speaking, is the equivalent of crucifixion, aka death to self. We are "*buried in His death.*" When we come to Christ, we must see ourselves as dead so that we can receive His life. Just praying a "*sinner's prayer*"—which isn't scriptural—is not the same as surrender. Surrender is death.

Think about it like this. When one drowns, it's because they can no longer breathe underwater. If they could, they'd save their own life. When they finally recognize they have no power to rescue themselves, they literally surrender their lives unto a watery death. When we take on Christ's baptism [water of the Word], we must visualize ourselves as "*going under.*" We are drowning our natural man because we have no power to save ourselves. In the spirit-realm, we baptize into death all that came from the bloodline of Adam. In this death condition, we are now available to take His new life. We are regenerated by a new bloodline from Jesus who is of Heaven. We take a brand new origin. We are no longer *"of the Earth"* but are *"of Heaven."* This is how we become *"strangers in the land of Earth."*

With this new origin, we must think from the vantage of our homeland, the Kingdom of God. This level of surrender causes a person to stop giving in to the temptations of the natural man, which brings us back to understanding we have but one nature while renting space in that of another nature. You are not your flesh or any of its feelings, desires, or temptations. When tempted with sexual sin [homosexuality, adultery, pornography, pedophilia, or fornication, bestiality], in any form, the flesh wants what it wants, no doubt. However, the surrendered spirit [the real you] within a human shell desires to please the One who gave him a new eternal life. In this condition, he will say *"No"* emphatically because he comprehends that life in the flesh is nothing short of despair, anguish, suffering, and destruction.

Drowning in Christ causes the newness. You cannot have newness without first "drowning." Many in the modern-day church preach. *"Accept Christ and then be baptized with water immersion."* However, Scriptures would indicate the opposite. We are to believe in the Father and Son unto salvation, be baptized into His Spirit, then water baptism may follow. The man on the cross received the Kingdom of Heaven through faith, yet was never water baptized. Unfortunately, we often misrepresent the purpose of baptism as if it's merely by water, or a prerequisite to receive God's Kingdom.

Grace and Repentance:

"Produce fruit in keeping with repentance (Matthew 3:8)."

"Three times I pleaded with the Lord to take it away from me. But He said to me, 'My grace is sufficient for you, for my power is made perfect in weakness.' Therefore I will all the more gladly boast about my weaknesses, so that Christ's power may rest on me (II Corinthians 12:8-9,)."

"For it is by grace you have been saved, through faith – and this is not from yourselves, it is the gift of God, not by works, so that no one can boast (Ephesians 2:8-9)."

Definition of Grace:
1. the free and unmerited favor of God, as manifested in the salvation of sinners and the bestowal of blessings
2. God giving you what you do not deserve (Heaven vs. hell; life vs. death; peace vs. chaos)
3. the catalyst for an otherwise impossible transformation from the old man of Adam to the new man in Christ

Definition of Repentance:
1. to turn from sin and dedicate oneself to the amendment of one's life
2. to feel regret or contrition *leading* to change one's mind
3. to cause to feel regret or contrition
4. to feel sorrow, regret, or contrition

Anyone who teaches grace outside repentance and surrender is a false teacher. Surrender and repentance are required to receive God's grace. Yes, we live in the Day of Grace, so it is extended to all mankind on a general level, but in respect to walking in personal grace regularly comes through a heart rent before a Holy God. In this condition of perpetual repentance of the sin-nature, His grace is surely sufficient for you and whatever situational crisis you may face.

When I write *"perpetual repentance,"* I mean walking continually in an attitude of cosigning all the lusts of the flesh unto God. It's as the Scripture directs, *"Being ready to punish all disobedience until personal obedience is achieved."* An attitude of repentance does *not* mean to self-abase, that is sin (Colossians 2:18, 23). Insulting, belittling, and beating oneself is self-abasement—that is not repentance. Repentance insists that you apologize to God for your action(s), go and sin no more, and continue unashamedly going about the Father's business. In true repentance, you are neither ashamed nor boastful in yourself because self is dead to the world and its lusts. Fruit of the Spirit of God can manifest only from a place of humility leading to repentance, which leads to grace.

Faith:

> "Now faith is confidence in what we hope for and assurance about what we do not see. This is what the ancients were commended for (Hebrews 11:1-2)."

> "Without faith it is impossible to please God (Hebrews 11:6)."

"Therefore, since we have been justified by faith, we have peace with God through our Lord Jesus Christ, through whom we have gained access by faith into this grace in which we now stand. And we boast in the hope of the glory of God (Romans 5:1-2)."

Faith is an extension of belief, but stronger than belief alone. Even the demons believe and shudder (James 2:19). Faith says, "*I not only believe You exist, but I place all my hope in You,*" unlike the demons. Faith moves the immovable, touches the untouchable, and makes the impossible possible.

Forgiveness:

"Therefore, my friends, I want you to know that through Jesus, the forgiveness of sins is proclaimed to you. Through Him, everyone who believes is set free from every sin, a justification you were not able to obtain under the law of Moses (Acts 13:38-39)."

Forgiveness has been extended by God through Jesus to all mankind, whether or not any of us receive it. It was granted to all mankind at the cross and resurrection of Christ. To receive it, all you must do is repent and it's yours. From there, the rest will come with great ease!

Repent to God. Accept His forgiveness. Forgive others. Let go of the shame, guilt, remorse, and condemnation. Let go of the lies, fear, doubt, and anxiety that lead you further and further into darkness.

A New Master!

"For sin shall no longer be your master, because you are not under the law, but under grace (Romans 6:14)."

"If the Son sets you free, you will be free indeed (John 8:36)."

"But now that you have been *set free from sin* and have become *slaves of God*, the benefit you reap leads to holiness, and the result is eternal life (Romans 6:22)."

"It is for freedom that Christ has set us free. Stand firm, then, and do not let yourselves be burdened again by a yoke of slavery (Galatians 5:1)."

"' I have the right to do anything,' you say – but not everything is beneficial. 'I have the right to do anything' – but I will not be mastered by anything (I Corinthians 6:12)."

"In him and through faith in him we may approach God with freedom and confidence (Ephesians 3:12)."

"You, my brothers and sisters, were called to be free. But do not use your freedom to indulge the flesh; rather, serve one another humbly in love. For the entire law is fulfilled in keeping this one command: 'Love your neighbor as yourself (Galatians 5:13-14).'"

Once you were alienated from God and were enemies in your minds because of your evil behavior. But now He has reconciled you by Christ's physical body through death to present you holy in His sight, without blemish and free from accusation – if you continue in your faith, established and firm, and do not move from the hope held out in the gospel. This is the gospel that you heard and that has been proclaimed to every creature under heaven, and of which I, Paul, have become a servant (Colossians 1:21-23)."

There is no greater gift from God than freedom! There is no greater pleasure or fulfillment in life than serving such a master because this Master is like no other. He is Father, Husband, Comforter, Healer, Redeemer, Forgiver. This is a master I can follow through eternity!

By surrendering to such a magnificent, loving God, you will begin to see that jumping from a ledge to *"end problems"* will no longer appear feasible. Its facade will no longer have the power to overtake you. In Christ, there is no greater place of peace, regardless of the storm, stemming from the liberty found only in knowing and consigning your life to Yahweh. That proverbial ledge will be revealed for what it is—of Satan.

Whatever mess you've concocted, whatever trial besets you, no matter what is happening or for whatever reason, when you submit unto death the nature of the flesh, God commands Himself to take what Satan means against you for evil and turn it for good. I've quoted this Scripture a million times over, yet I will continue to do so because many folks still don't get it. In Christ, there is no dilemma, only benefits from His Kingdom solution. Every horrible, disastrous, despicable situation is a platform God utilizes to catapult His people onto higher ground.

For more detailed information on this matter, I suggest reading the Bible beginning with the gospels to follow the life of Christ, the One who overcame death, grave, and every temptation known to man. He overcame the flesh while living in it. Once He is allowed to take over your life, you too will be able to do as He because His completed work will begin to manifest through you. Additionally, I have written numerous books elaborating on the subjects of knowing your identity in Christ, who you are in the Kingdom of God, how to draw closer to the heart of God, and much more.

If you learn nothing else from this, know that God is in love with you and always will be. He formed you in your mother's womb. He allowed your life to be spared thus far. There is life beyond this crisis. There is joy beyond this sorrow. There is acceptance beyond your rejections. There is gain after your loss. There is life outside death. Be encouraged and of good cheer, for Christ is in love with you today!

Author's Catalog

What was God Thinking?

Looking for God, 3 volumes or complete series

Discovering the Person of Holy Spirit, 4 volumes or complete series

How to Get it Right: Being Single, Married, Divorced and Everything in Between

Thy Kingdom Come: Kingdom vs. Religion

Holiness or Heresy: The Modern-Day Church

Navigating the Fiery Black Holes of Life: A Book of Faith

Talking Yourself off the Ledge: Encouragement at a Glance

Walking the Path of Freedom

When All My Strength has Failed

Wielding the Sword of the Spirit

Learning to Digest the Truth

Marriage Beyond Mediocrity

Wise as a Serpent, Innocent as a Dove

Philadelphia

Casting

Extinguishing the Inferno of Anger

Wrecked by My Ex

The War

Understanding Kingdom Prayer

Out of Obscurity

Gauchos, God, and Great Expectations

The Fiery Sword Global Ministries

The Fiery Sword Publications

Lexington, SC 29073

www.thefierysword.com

thefierysword@windstream.net

Made in the USA
Columbia, SC
25 September 2022

67915085R00107